Out of the Mouths of Babes

Out of the Mouths of Babes:

Parenting from a Child's Perspective

DYAN EYBERGEN

Shannon
yours in parenting
Enjoy!!
Dyan Eybergen

iUniverse, Inc.
New York   Bloomington

Out of the Mouths of Babes
Parenting from a Child's Perspective

iUniverse books may be ordered through booksellers or by contacting:

iUniverse
1663 Liberty Drive
Bloomington, IN 47403
www.iuniverse.com
1-800-Authors (1-800-288-4677)

Because of the dynamic nature of the Internet, any Web addresses or links
contained in this book may have changed since publication and may no longer
be valid. The views expressed in this work are solely those of the author and
do not necessarily reflect the views of the publisher, and the publisher hereby
disclaims any responsibility for them.

ISBN: 978-0-595-47062-4 (pbk)
ISBN: 978-0-595-49754-6 (cloth)
ISBN: 978-0-595-91344-2 (ebk)

Printed in the United States of America

For Mom and Dad:
my mentors in parenting

and

Shae Calhoun:
for inspiring the fear out of me

I had a dream of you last night,
You were hanging stars from trees,
A red one, a blue one and a yellow one.
You were like a mommy princess.
I drew a circle around you,
And Daddy came, and you married him,
And I was your baby.

Talen, age 4

In the interest of simplicity, I have opted to use only masculine pronouns (he, him, his). They are, of course, meant to refer to both boys and girls.

Contents

Acknowledgements

My special thanks to the team at iUniverse for helping to make my dream come true.

Love, hugs and kisses go out to my boys, Kohan, Nolan and Talen. You have been my inspiration for so much in life. Writing *Out of the Mouths of Babes* personifies just how much. These pages are your memoirs. I hope it makes up for all the information I neglected to write down in each of your baby memory books.

I am so grateful for all the wisdom that has been bestowed upon me from out of the mouths of babes. Every time I hear a child verbalize something that expresses his point of view, my world is altered. Thank you, Kohan, Nolan, Talen, Adam, Daryan, Keldan, Vanesa, Cameron, Ava, Vicki, Caitlyn, Myles, Rheanna, Alana, Lilly, Emily and Madelyn; every chapter in this book was inspired by the words each of you said. (Evan, please don't feel left out. You have provided me with more than enough material to write the sequel: *Parenting from a Teenager's Perspective*. I thank you in advance.)

There have been some phenomenal women who allowed me to share their stories to help put the child's viewpoint into perspective. I offer many thanks to Vicki Train, Karen Makela, Holly Davidson, Sandra Street, Connie Kenny and Ashley Casey. I couldn't have paralleled the situational experiences between children and adults any better if I had made them up myself. Your stories have been invaluable to this project.

So many people embraced my vision for this book and encouraged my writing. Jane Hook, as you sculpted, you listened for hours as I read you chapter after chapter. I always marvel at how you were able to concentrate so intently on my reading and still sculpt something so beautiful. Your enthusiasm and belief in my ability to write this book overwhelm me. Karen Makela, my wonderful sister, I could draw a line on a page, and you would say it was the best damn thing! Your support sustains me. Vicki Train, my other wonderful sister, I am sincerely honoured that this will be the first book you ever read. Your undying friendship and faith in my capabilities nourish me. Jane Eybergen, thanks for asking the question, "Why would I buy your book over anyone else's?" John Slater, your unwavering interest in my writing fuelled the engine that could. Deanna Casey, even during some of the darkest times, you found a way to be happy for me. I can always count on you to be in my corner. Deb Dejong, I am so grateful to you and KW Counselling for providing me with so many opportunities to educate other parents. Writing and publishing your book *Dance* ignited the courage within me to get started. Michaela Danhousen, thanks for taking part of my manuscript with you on your trip to Florida—I have never thought of it as beach material, but when you said it grabbed your attention, I was encouraged to keep writing. Grand River Writer's Circle—this little, eclectic group gave honest, insightful feedback. I have no doubt we will all be published one day. Sandra Street, my sista-friend, I know I can always toot my horn when I'm with you. Phil Dwyer, no matter what happens, I will always have that first glowing review. Shelley Ali, you came to me in the eleventh hour; your design creativity made it all tangible. Barbara Dyzuk, I am indebted to you for giving me the opportunity to work as a parent educator. I became a better parent as a result of my learnings as a facilitator. When you came around years later and read some of what I wrote, it was your opinion that I valued the most.

I would be remiss if I did not mention the writers who

came before and influenced me: Selma H. Fraiberg, Alicia F. Lieberman, Barbara Coloroso, Iris Krasnow, Gordon Neufeld, Katrina Kenison, Noah Lukeman, Barbara DeMarco-Barrett, Susan Driscoll and Diane Gedyman. Each of your works helped me to create my own. I am forever grateful for your knowledge and wisdom.

I have not lived the content of this book on my own. My husband, Rob Eybergen, has been with me every step of the way. There is no one else I would rather travel with along this parenting journey. You light the way when I am searching in darkness. The boys will never question how much you love them; you say it in everything you do.

Preface

As a registered nurse working with psychiatric children and adolescents, there wasn't a behavioural situation I wasn't trained to handle—until I had my own children. All my education and years of experience did nothing to prepare me for the intensity of the relationship I would have with my sons: the profound love I would have for each of them, the anger I could feel toward them sometimes, the immense joy of watching them grow and discover new things and the *guilt*.

I gave birth to the idea of this book the day my first son was born, and for the last 10 years have parented my way into writing it. In honour of the past decade, I have chronicled the lives of my children thus far and have bound their stories within these pages. The chapters narrate my experience as a mother of three boys—how my husband and I learned to parent them as unique individuals, and how we cultivated our style of parenting derived from the philosophy of attachment theory. Every child-care topic featured in *Out of the Mouths of Babes* relates to an adult situation that invites parents to develop a respectful understanding for their child's point of view. The quotations by young children shared throughout are treasured memories of some of the profound things our boys have said over the years. Some references have been told to me by family and friends and some are from parents who attended workshops I facilitated through KW Counselling. All of them help put into perspective how children see the world around them.

I truly believe that when we respond to our child's perception, and take into consideration his unique personality and stage of development, we safeguard ourselves against making horrible parenting mistakes, like spanking when we swore we never would, or making derogatory comments that are too harsh to be forgotten. My hope is that the words and stories from *Out of the Mouths of Babes* will give light to someone else's parenting journey in the same way they have illuminated a path for my husband and me.

Dyan Eybergen
February 2008

Introduction

The first period of childhood, roughly the first five years of life, is submerged like a buried city, and when we come back to these times with our children we are strangers and we cannot easily find our way.
Selma H. Fraiberg
The Magic Years

Visiting a bookstore in search of child-rearing wisdom can be an overwhelming endeavour. There are thousands of how-to parenting books to choose from, and with so many theories and quick-fix solutions to parenting dilemmas being offered, it's hard to know the right choice. What my husband and I discovered (after spending a small fortune on parenting resources) was that more often than not, we had to modify suggested parenting book strategies to meet the individual needs of our three sons. What worked in one instance with one child rarely brought forward the same results with another. Our three boys are *so* different in terms of their personalities and temperaments. It made sense for us to parent them differently by attuning to their individuality. When my husband and I consciously worked with each child's unique personality, we found we got more favourable results than if we tried to parent from a one-size-fits-all paradigm.

My husband and I defaulted to the principles of attachment theory purely by instinct. When our boys were babies, it was relatively easy to respond to the cues they gave us—they cried when they were hungry, wet or tired, and we acted accordingly.

I breast-fed on demand, we rocked crying infants, changed their diapers frequently, echoed their coos and held them a lot—it seemed like the natural thing to do. Through our studies in psychology and my vocation as a psychiatric nurse, we had a good understanding of the theory of attachment but hadn't thought of its application in terms of parenting through tantrums, toilet training and sibling rivalry, or school conflicts. Unfortunately, books available on attachment parenting at the time were limited and rarely discussed raising children past the toddler stage. When our children became preschool age, we had to stretch the theories' principles to come up with parenting solutions to bedtime fears, misbehaviour, finicky eaters and the like. Keeping the premise of attachment theory at the forefront of our actions, we found ways to parent through these challenges that complemented each child's distinct personality.

The theory of attachment came out of the extensive research conducted in the 1950s by an English psychiatrist, John Bowlby. Mary Ainsworth, an American psychologist, later brought Bowlby's theory to the United States and developed a method of assessing infant attachment. This duo defined attachment in behavioural, emotional and psychobiological terms: babies are born with the capacity to feel deep emotions such as separation, excitement and sadness; however, they have little capability for understanding or regulating the intensity of these emotions and rely on caregivers to help them feel comfort and security. A baby will form a bond with his caregiver when he trusts that that person will respond to his attempts to interrelate with him. The quality of attachment evolves over time, as the infant's opportunity to interact with his caregiver increases and those interactions are positive in nature. Children who are healthily attached grow to safely explore the world around them, become less overwhelmed by extreme emotions and learn to normalize intense feelings, resulting in a state of equilibrium.

In his book entitled *The First Relationship: Infant and Mother*, Daniel N. Stern (2002), a noted psychiatrist in the field of parent-infant psychotherapy, expressed that both the mother's and infant's behaviours are reciprocal exchanges in an effort to regulate the baby's momentary state. Dr. William Sears, author of numerous parenting books rooted in the principles of attachment theory, concurs with Stern and explains attachment parenting as a cyclical process where parents suitably respond to the cues their child gives them, the child feels valued and learns how to give better indications for his needs and wants, and in turn the parents learn to answer more appropriately, and so on.

When our children's personalities diverge from infancy, and their emotional and physical requirements broaden beyond needing to be changed, fed or lulled to sleep, it becomes increasingly more difficult for parents to understand the ambiguity of a child's behaviour and respond in a way that is right for a particular child. Our ability to attune as parents depends largely on the temperament of the child, as well as his stage of development. Attachment parenting can also be affected by whether or not the parent can relate to a particular child, given the parent's own personality traits and family of origin entrenchments. Whether it is an infant who is a reluctant sleeper, a preschooler who refuses to eat, or a school-aged child plagued with fear, it can be immensely challenging trying to cope when we have little understanding for why the child is behaving in an undesirable way, and the child has little insight as to why he is misbehaving and can't explain it either.

Often we get caught up in the emotional exchange between ourselves and our children and react impulsively, only to regret our actions later. As parents, we can't always remember what it felt like to be children—especially during emotionally trying times. But we *can* develop an understanding of how our children are thinking and feeling by paralleling their experience with our own. If we step back, slow down our reaction time and think of ourselves in the same situation, we create a moment where we are vulnerable to understanding and open to appreciating how the child is affected by what is happening. We begin to see the experience of the child through his eyes. *Understanding* buffers emotionally charged reactions; it equips us with the rational tools needed to respond appropriately, and, in doing so, the child's integrity remains intact. The parents gain confidence in their parenting, and the child is assisted to develop a healthy self-esteem. As a result, the parent and child cultivate a mutually respectful bond.

Attachment parenting is like software protection: if you do not continue to subscribe to its application, a virus will creep in and destroy your entire system, rendering it dysfunctional.

1
Bedtime and Sleeping through the Night

"Only kids can come; that means Mommy can't come."
"Mommy can come, Kohan; Mommy is a kid."
"If Mommy were a kid, Nolan, she would sleep in a little bed."
Kohan, age 6
Nolan, age 4

Our eldest son slept through the night on his own three weeks after he was born. I would like to say it was because of some wonderful magical bedtime strategy my husband and I conjured up and that this chapter is devoted to bestowing that wisdom, but the truth of the matter is we had nothing to do with it. Our first baby was inherently self-reliant in comforting himself; he was a thumb sucker. Laying him down in the crib was an automatic cue for him to insert thumb in mouth. His eyes would instantly roll back to the lull of his own sucking, and he would fall asleep within a few minutes. This proved a more powerful sedative than any amount of rocking, breast-feeding or trips around the block in the car. As new parents, we took much pride in how well our child slept. I am convinced the triumph over telling envious friends that our infant was sleeping 10 to 12 hours a night was the catalyst for having two more children. Our nemesis: those next two babies gave us a rude awakening—and I use the word *awakening* in the most literal sense.

Our second-born came out of my womb hungry and ate every two hours for the next six months. A power-snooze lasting

20 to 40 minutes was all I could hope for during the day. This boy never slept when it was convenient for me, nor did he time his slumber to coincide with his older brother's afternoon naps. Every time he closed his eyes during the day, I would take the opportunity to get some housework underway. The dishwasher was permanently half emptied, and clean laundry sat in baskets for weeks. One day, while dozing in his car seat, cozy beside the fireplace, I was desperate to get some much-needed housecleaning done. For some absurd reason, I began my pursuit of domestic bliss by wiping the mantle above where he slept. Manoeuvring around the car seat on tiptoe to dust objects well beyond my reach, I bumped a ceramic angel off the mantle, knocking my four-week-old baby unconscious and giving him a concussion. Just imagine explaining that one in the emergency room.

If my days weren't arduous enough with a toddler and a newborn who didn't sleep, the nights were especially exhausting. The baby would go down well after midnight, and he never stayed asleep longer than two or three hours. We sacrificed all the rules of getting a child to sleep through the night in exchange for some REM of my own. I nursed in bed, rolling over when it was time to feed again at two-hour intervals; we rocked and sang that baby to sleep and responded to his cries through the night by bringing him into bed with us. We thought we were creating bad habits and had no one to blame but ourselves when he did not sleep through the night on his own until he was three-and-a-half. At that time, I told him I was going to live in a hotel if he continued getting out of bed. I have visions of him now at eight years old, hiding under his covers too afraid to call out for me, as I may start packing my bags for the nearest Holiday Inn. I was pregnant with my third child and could no longer stand being in the hypnotic zone of sleep deprivation. Soon I would be getting up during the night with an infant. I could only pray our third baby was going to be a sleeper. He wasn't, of course. He was actually worse.

Our youngest son never slept during the day, and he cried

incessantly. Determined not to have another child succumb to the bad sleep habits we thought our poor parenting had created, we vowed to do things differently. When he was six months of age, we tried the Ferber method: Dr. Richard Ferber (2006) instructs parents to pat and comfort their baby at timed intervals, but not to pick up or feed him. We started by going to check and reassure him every five minutes and would gradually increase the time in between checks until he fell asleep. The theory is, after a few days to a week, most babies learn to fall asleep on their own. After eight days of not going to bed myself until four in the morning (when he finally stopped crying), we felt we had no other choice but to research other methods.

I read about desensitization in a parenting magazine. This approach suggests the parent lay the infant down in his crib fully awake. The parent is then instructed to take a seat in the baby's room but is advised not to react to the little one's cries by talking to or looking at him. The child feels comforted by the fact that he can see the parent but learns that his attempts to get Mom or Dad to pick him up are futile. Eventually, he will fall asleep. *Eventually*— how long is that, exactly? These arbitrary words meaning in "due course" or "sooner or later," are highly sensitive to individual response. *Eventually* may mean 10 days for our child, and *ultimately* may mean three days for someone else's. I sat there, night after night, hour after hour, with a blank expression on my face until I couldn't take it any longer and would burst into tears myself.

My husband and I tried other strategies to help our baby sleep through the night, all to no avail. I know these methods have proved successful for many families. Unfortunately, we could not seem to find the one solution that worked for us within a reasonable amount of time, despite our best efforts. I have questioned whether consistency was an issue. I am certain we were consistent for as long as we were using each strategy. It was the length of time we needed to invest in each technique that was too difficult for us. We thought it cruel to let our baby cry for hours every night when we had no idea how much time needed to pass before the new bedtime routine took effect. We reverted back to our old parenting ways of rocking, coddling, soothing and bringing that little tot into bed with us. It was less anxiety-provoking for me, and our baby seemed more content. He is now three-and-a-half, and as you probably guessed, he is not consistently sleeping through the night on his own.

"Mommy, you love me so you should stay and sleep in my bed."
"But I love Daddy too."
"Well, Daddy's not little!"

Talen, age 4
Mother, age 30-something

For the longest time, I thought our two sons were anomalies and that my husband and I failed miserably in training them to sleep independently. When I started out as a parent educator, I was enlightened by the numerous stories I heard from frustrated parents who also had difficulty conquering their child's will in this regard. Then I came across a *Today's Parent* (Spicer 2003) magazine article citing a 1999 *New Yorker* interview with Dr. Richard Ferber where he recanted by saying: "There are some children you just cannot train to sleep through the night—they just won't stop crying." What an immense relief. Our children were not freaks of nature after all. When I realized we were not alone in this challenge, I began thinking about it differently. Perhaps we hadn't failed as parents; perhaps it had more to do with our children's natural dispositions. I was more than willing to accept this hypothesis; it certainly got me off the hook when well-meaning grandparents insisted we "let him cry it out." I reluctantly agreed once and left our youngest with my father, who later said to me that he had never heard anything like it: "He cries like he is having a limb amputated, and he won't stop until you go and get him." Never has there been a more tempting time to say, "I told you so."

There are explanations inherent to temperament that makes some children resistant to the interventions we use to get them to sleep on their own. American psychiatrists Stella Chess and Alexander Thomas confronted the nature-nurture dichotomy and began looking at temperament traits in 1956. Collecting longitudinal data from over 100 children and following them from infancy through early adulthood, Chess and Thomas identified nine basic temperament traits that affect everything a child does from eating to sleeping to learning to use the toilet. They categorized these nine traits into three major temperamental types: easy, difficult and slow to adapt. Some children, like our first-born, have a natural contented demeanor. It takes little to no effort at all on behalf of the parents to get an *easy* child to sleep. Other children need to be nurtured into feeling secure so they can *eventually* learn to sleep independently; according to Thomas and Chess, these children would be considered *difficult* or *slow to adapt*.

As a family educator, I am often asked what else can be done when all the contemporary methods have not worked. The objective remains the same for all children—regardless if they are difficult or slow to adapt—the road to getting there is just inevitably longer. We want our babies to develop an inner sense of well-being so they feel secure enough to stay in their own beds all night. And let's face it; we parents need some sleep too. We have to learn to work with our child's uniqueness and not try to fix him according to our idea of who he should be. By anticipating the needs of our children based on the character traits they possess, parents can reduce the stress of bedtime for all those concerned. I encourage parents to *try on* their child's temperament and think about how they would like to be treated in the same circumstance. I find it helpful to lend some understanding to any parent-child conflict by telling a story about an adult experience that parallels that of the child's. Although many of my comparisons seem preposterous in nature and are often quite laughable, they assist to evoke feelings of empathy for the child. When we can relate to the child's perception of any given experience, we are better equipped to customize our response and deal with it in a supportive way.

My husband and I attended a social function not that long ago. It was an awkward affair, and we were nervous about going. During the evening, a conversation I was having with a family member went in a direction that should have been off-limits, and an argument ensued. I had my feelings hurt terribly, and as a result I left the party early. My husband stayed behind for what felt like an eternity to try and salvage impaired relations. I returned home, crashed down on the bed and began to cry. The longer it took for him to come back from the party, the more distraught I became. When finally he crawled in beside me and enfolded me in his arms, and I felt the sustenance of his love and understanding, I was able to calm myself, and in time I fell asleep. I could not have slept alone that night; I needed to be consoled. If my husband had not come back to check on me, I would have assumed he didn't care that I was hurting. If he hadn't stayed with me when he did return, I would have felt abandoned. Babies cannot formulate these types of emotions into words, but their responses to their parents leaving them are indicative of similar feelings.

When I equate our children's need for solace during the night with my own recent experience of being too upset to fall asleep by myself, I can appreciate their temperament all the more and have little regret about responding to them the way we did. I admit it would have been less exhausting to have successfully exercised one of the strategies to get both our boys to sleep through the night at a much earlier age than three-and-a-half. The dark circles under my eyes are a true testament to that. However, we chose instead to surrender to our children's innate desire to feel comfort. When we adults need reassurance and understanding, the last thing we expect is for people to ignore us. Parents' response to the needs of their children, in any given situation, should be no different from the response they would expect for themselves.

*"It's not fair! Big people like mommies and daddies
sleep together, and little people who are scared have
to sleep alone."*

Daryan, age 4

When he was 18 months, our eldest son had a bout with night terrors, a phenomenon characterized by a sudden arousal from the deepest sleep with a piercing scream or cry, accompanied by behavioural manifestations of intense fear, which last anywhere from five to twenty minutes. The child is generally still asleep when the night terrors occur and has no memory of them upon waking the next morning. The first time it happened, I was thunderstruck as to what to do. Our son was unresponsive to our efforts to calm him, and he thwarted any physical contact we tried to make by thrashing his arms and legs into the air. He was covered in sweat, and he contorted his body in a wasted attempt to escape the terror within his mind.

It's unnerving to watch your child battle against a formidable threat that only he can see; the time it took to subside felt endless. When it was over, he put his head back down on the pillow and resumed sleep as if nothing had transpired.

There were no logical explanations for why this was happening to our son. He had not been exposed to any trauma that we were aware of, and there had been no substantial changes to his routine. This was a happy, contented toddler who had always been a good sleeper. My husband and I were relieved to learn that episodic night terrors in children are normal—often brought on by overtiredness—and do not suggest psychological problems. They are usually transient and go away on their own. Once we had a better understanding of what was happening, it was easier to deal with in a more altruistic way. If a nap did not take place during the day, we imposed an earlier bedtime. If a night terror occurred, we were careful not to wake him, we ensured his safety and we avoided stressing him by talking loudly or insisting he go back to bed. We simply let the attack run its course until the panic diminished. The more adept we became at handling each episode, the less intense the night terror appeared. It was a blip in our child's sleep pattern that lasted just shy of two months. He's 11 years old now and continues to sleep like he did when he was a baby (with the exception of sucking his thumb).

Nightmares proved to be more intrusive for our family. Unlike night terrors, the child can usually recall what he dreamt and often associates the demons he dreams about with his bedroom. Our younger two sons were frequently the prey of whatever went bump in the night, making bedtime an immense challenge. Our middle child was particularly tormented by nightmares and could give elaborate details upon waking, which began to also preoccupy much of his thoughts during the day. Even though we insisted there were no poltergeists living in his room, we felt compelled to try "Monster Spray," a "magic wand" and a dream catcher, in an effort to placate our son's fears. Some of these things worked some of the time, but more often than not, my husband and I would have him visit our bed during the night. My husband also tried lying with our son before bed, and they would make up versions of the dream where Daddy would fight off the evil monsters; we thought that if we created an alternate ending where our son was saved by his father, then the nightmares would stop. This tactic certainly helped our son feel better about going to sleep but didn't prevent the bad dreams from happening.

I can't give a better example of where taking the child's lead in finding a solution had the biggest impact, than in this particular situation. We purchased bunk beds for our boys' room and naturally, due to safety concerns, had him sleeping in the lower bed. Our son thought that if he slept up top he would be farther away from the monsters and less likely to be seen by them. Since being allowed to sleep on the upper bunk he has had considerably fewer nightmares and our bedtime routine is less problematic.

"I don't like to sleep in my room; monsters live in there."
Talen, age 3

When our youngest began having bad dreams, we tried the one-solution-fits-all approach and were reminded very quickly that different temperaments require specialized responses. This child differs from our middle son in that he is less inclined to persistently worry and is comforted through touch more than through the spoken word. We want to empower him to find his own answer to solving this problem, but for right now he insists the only remedy is to sleep in Mommy and Daddy's bed. When he comes to us in the middle of the night and says monsters are after him, we scoop him up, give him a quick snuggle and gently guide him back to his own room. A hug and a few kisses seem to be enough, as he usually doesn't protest returning to his bed. When we have been adamant about not letting him come to our room, we found the crying and carrying on lasted much longer; the other two boys would unavoidably wake up, and everybody would be deprived of sleep.

It's a delicate balance between feeding into behavioural antics and providing reassurance. Sometimes, the child is defiant because he is reluctant to give up the fun he was having during the day in exchange for boredom between the sheets. The predicament is in discerning if your child is genuinely afraid of something or just not ready to go to bed. You have to determine what the underlying cause of his behaviour is so you can tailor your reaction to meet the child's need, all the while advancing toward the ultimate goal of getting that child to sleep independently. My husband and I couple our response with some direction for how our son can calm himself, and we applaud his efforts when he does try. As time goes on, we are having fewer interruptions to our sleep, and our little guy is so proud when he does make it through the night on his own. It's a work in progress, but we're getting there.

When we relocated to a new house, my two sisters came to help. After a long day of moving and rearranging furniture, we celebrated the acquisition of our first home with pizza and champagne and went to bed late. My sisters retired to the basement and slept on an inflatable mattress. In the wee hours before dawn, my middle sister had a dream she was being accosted by a stranger. She was yelling out in her sleep, and our eldest sibling tried to shake her awake, so when she opened her eyes, she saw our eldest sister as the silhouette of a stranger looming over her. Being in a strange place, she temporarily had no recollection of where she was or whom she was with; any attempts to calm her were refuted by her kicking and screaming. In the darkness, she found her way up the stairs and entered the master bedroom where my husband and I were sleeping. It is worth noting that my husband sleeps in the nude—it lends itself to the incredulity of this situation. My sister, at 34 years of age, was so freaked out that she jumped onto our bed, got under the sheets and lay down in between my naked husband and myself. She felt traumatized and had no intention of returning to the basement until the sun came up. It was difficult for my husband to get out of bed to put clothes on; it was a small room, and one side of the bed was tight against the wall. He slept on that side, making it impossible to get out without having to crawl over my sister and me. The only appropriate thing to do was for the three of us to remain lying next to each other for the few hours left until morning.

When I reference the adult experience of being too afraid to sleep alone because of bad thoughts, scary noises or disturbing dreams, I have a better appreciation for the child's perception. The example of my sister's frightening dream is one of many that I am aware of among my adult friends and family. My eldest sister cannot sleep by herself when it is thundering and lightning. Our neighbour has had her mother sleeping on her couch every night since her husband passed away over a year ago because she is too afraid to be alone. A friend cannot stay in her home at night when her husband is away on business—she packs the kids up and retreats to her parents. Another friend needs to sleep with the TV on because she gets spooked by the sounds her house makes at night.

As adults, we have had years to build a repertoire of coping skills and self-calming techniques, yet so many of us depend on the relief in knowing that when we wake up afraid, we have someone sleeping close to us who ensures our safety. How can we expect then, when it's dark and they are alone, that these little people should know how to manage frightening dreams and upsetting ideas better than most of us do? If we're not doing a good job of handling night-time fears or sentiments of loneliness, then we can only expect our children to learn from our example. It is imperative, then, that we model appropriate coping strategies for our children and help them to implement ones of their own.

"No, I'm not tired! I always yawn, but I never fall asleep."
Nolan, age 8

My husband decided to build a sleep camp in the backyard at our cottage. It was to be a worthwhile project. When the extended family got together, there wasn't enough room for everyone to sleep without invading one another's privacy. It was also difficult for adults to stay up late without inevitably waking one of the children. (Everyone knows what a damper that can put on a good party.) A child who has been aroused by the loud goings-on of his parents is never eager to fall back asleep, in fear that he might miss something fun. This building provided a space where the kids could hang out, particularly on rainy days when cabin fever ran rampant among those under 12 years of age, and madness afflicted anyone over 20. It was liberating to send rambunctious children out to the *bunky*—as we affectionately called it—whenever the noise reached an intolerable level. The extra space also provided much-needed sleeping room, with two sets of bunk beds and a pullout. Equipped with walkie-talkies for emergency purposes only, the four oldest cousins were elated to camp out in the bunky a few feet away from the main cottage.

We adults reclaimed our space and relished the fact that each of us actually got to sleep in a bedroom with a door. Early morning awakenings to high-pitched giggles and clanking cereal bowls were a thing of the past. The kids stayed out until they were hungry enough to come in, which usually gave the adults an extra hour in dreamland.

It was all going according to plan until the eldest of the four children decided to introduce ghost stories as the favoured source of bedtime entertainment. The same urban legends told to us when we were young were now being heard by this new generation. Our second son was only six years old at the time. We had been so careful to censor what our boys watched on TV or DVD; it never occurred to us that his first exposure to the horror genre would be through any means other than visual media. He was far too young and impressionable to be subjected to that kind of storytelling. In hindsight, this child should have been sleeping in the main cottage until he was older. It's been two years, and he has yet to return to the bunky to sleep with the other children. He wants to. He begins each day of his vacation saying, "Tonight I feel that I can stay out there; I'm really going to do it this time." And every night before bed, he changes his mind. He's frustrated and disappointed in himself. He doesn't want to be afraid and certainly doesn't want his cousins or his brother to think he is. It has not been helpful to minimize or dismiss his concerns; he becomes quite cantankerous when people suggest he should not worry so much about it. The phobia is bigger than he is right now. Through empowerment and praise in his effort to conquer, he is beginning to build courage. Every incremental step—from just thinking he can stay in the bunky to actually managing to sleep out there accompanied by an adult—brings him closer to taking back the control that fear stole from him.

I bent the panelling back from the wall in my room, of that very same cottage, when I was about five or six years old, to spy on my parents watching a movie. I witnessed a scene in the film where a young woman found a dead man's body floating in her bathtub. Hysterically, she ran to the house next door to find help, and when she returned, accompanied by the neighbour, they found instead of a dead body, a Raggedy Ann doll immersed in the bath water. I had one of those dolls—with a heart tattooed on her chest with the words "I love you" written inside. I packed it away in a cedar chest, never to be resurrected, after seeing that disturbing film. I spent the following few nights snuggled between my mother and father in their bed. It's been 35 years, and I can still recall how frightened I was to stay in my own room. I can't remember what they did to get me to sleep on my own again, but I do know that it wasn't by suggesting I camp out in the backyard.

Just as Raggedy Ann has a negative connotation for me, so does the bunky for our son. To insist he stay out there before he is ready could be quite detrimental to his psyche. No one wants to feel scared, and certainly no one wants to feel scared and have to sleep in a place that feels unsafe.

2
Toilet Training

"Mommy, why doesn't your bum fit into the toilet?"
Adam, age 3

Almost everything I learned about instructing a child to use the toilet I acquired through the teachings of my eldest son. He decided when it was time to get out of diapers and into big boy underwear before I even thought about initiating the process of potty training. It wasn't a conscious plan to wait until he did it on his own—he was only two years old—it just happened that way.

Being a first-time mother, I hadn't a clue as to how or when I should start teaching our son to use the toilet. A background in nursing provided me with the fundamental concepts of bladder and bowel development: I understood that in an infant, the automatic involuntary mechanism involved in contracting the smooth muscles of the bladder and bowel is controlled by the sympathetic nervous system. As a child's nervous and excretory systems mature, this automatic mechanism is replaced by a voluntary one, making conscious control over elimination possible. It is a highly individualized maturation process, and accurately evaluating whether or not a child's excretory system is developed enough can be challenging. Some children present with signs of readiness between two and three years, and others not until much later. There are overt signs that are helpful in predicting physical and emotional readiness: the child shows interest in what you are doing in the bathroom; he shows a preference for a clean, dry diaper; the child feels the sensation of having to urinate or have a bowel movement seconds prior to going; he can tell you he has gone; the child is often dry after waking from a nap; the number of diapers he is using during the day declines dramatically; he has the manual dexterity to pull his pants up and down; the child will find a private place, such as a corner or behind furniture, to have a bowel movement; or the child may start refusing to go in his diaper.

In hindsight, I realize our son demonstrated many of these behaviours prior to relinquishing his use of diapers. The most significant for him was constipation. Not cognizant of these precursors at the time, it was surprising when he came to me one day and asked to wear underwear like Daddy. With a newborn at home that rarely slept, I felt tired and lacking in patience. It took some serious consideration whether or not to take this on. In an effort to dissuade him, I explained that his skin would no longer be protected with diapers and that going in his pants would feel wet and sticky. I cautioned him that he would have to use the toilet and that that was a "big boy" responsibility. He looked at me rather incredulously and said (not in so many words) that was indeed the plan. His determination was convincing in spite of my unwillingness, so in an effort not to impede his enthusiasm, we made the trip to a department store that afternoon. During the drive, I couldn't help but wonder how I was going to manage. I couldn't fathom having to endure public accidents, getting up in the middle of the night to wash soiled bedsheets, or having the energy to encourage this little tyke along his developmental journey. I felt ill-equipped in knowledge and stamina. I thought it might be a good idea to stop by the library on our way home and find some information on the do's and don'ts of toilet training. If we were going to do this, we should do it the right way the first time.

We found our way to the boys' section of the store and, after spending a considerable amount of time deliberating over numerous trade brands, our son decided on a six-pack of superhero briefs. His excitement was hard to contain. If I had allowed it, he would have ripped off his diaper in the checkout aisle and put on a pair of those new undies right then and there. We agreed to wait until we got home, postponing our trip to the library. A nagging toddler is not conducive to doing research. I thought I would have months of trials and tribulations anyway; one day without a reference book was not going to make a difference. Ironically, I had no use for *Toilet Training for Dummies*. From the moment we changed into those first pair of Spiderman underpants, he demonstrated proficiency at using the toilet. Our son gained control of his bladder and bowels during the day and night in literally that one 24-hour period, and his problem with constipation instantaneously resolved. I can count on one hand how many accidents he had.

Thinking that our good fortune in not having to go through the daunting task of potty training was just a fluke, we never expected our second-born to establish the same independence in learning to use the toilet as his brother had done. We were pleasantly amazed when his experience was the equivalent to our eldest boy's. By the time our middle child was two years old, he began to resist diaper changes with fierce determination. He would squirm and wriggle until he released himself from the Velcro hold of a clean diaper and delighted in the freedom of running around naked. During one of these streaker episodes, he climbed up and sat on the toilet announcing, "My do like brover do," and he went for the first time. The sense of pride he felt in this accomplishment provoked the refusal to use diapers from that point on. Like his brother, he established mastery over bladder and bowel control during the day and night in a matter of one day. He also had very few accidents.

"Here, Keldan, let Grandma help you."
"Grandma, have you ever seen a bum before?"
Grandma, age 50-something
Keldan, age 3

Having always considered that the role of parent was synonymous with teacher, I am humbled by the role reversal that happened here between me and my boys. Not having a plan for how to initiate the process of toilet training, I was fated to take their lead. In doing so, I became educated on the reliability of the natural progression of physical development. We do not feed an infant solid food before his digestive system matures, we do not coax teething to occur and we cannot make a child walk before he has gross motor capability. Parental intervention (with the exception of providing good nutrition for healthy growth and development) is not necessary for any of these biological milestones to take place. Yet as a society we are so eager to force the physiological maturation of our children's excretory systems before voluntary control is established. If toilet teaching is commenced before regulation of the muscles responsible for elimination has occurred, the parent is only training reflexes—like Pavlov's dogs that learned to salivate at hearing the ringing of a bell.

Proponents of early infant training repeatedly hold a babe over the toilet to condition urinary or bowel reactions to occur—the parent is trained, not the child. You cannot expect an infant to take the initiative to do this on his own before he is physically competent. The only advantage I can see to this is the task of cleaning dirty diapers is dramatically reduced, and the cost of disposables is brought to a nominal amount. Although I recognize the importance of these issues, the last thing I would want to do is hold my son over the toilet for an indefinite amount of time, several times a day, waiting for him to perform his duty. In addition to this labourious commitment, I know I wouldn't appreciate being forced to do something I wasn't ready to do, and therefore I cannot support coercing a child. Our family conceded to the work of cloth diapers at home during the day and budgeted accordingly for the use of disposables at night and on outings. Although this compromise worked well for us on a pragmatic front, we would be lackadaisical parents if we didn't reflect on whether or not it served us ethically. After mulling over the practical issues of choosing one method over another, it is equally important to consider the emotional ramifications of a choice. The criticism often associated with training a child when he is older is that it is cruel to let a child beyond two years of age "sit" in a soiled diaper. We would never have let our sons "sit" in wet, stinky pants—we felt obliged to change them right away. I cannot imagine any parent *wanting* a child to be uncomfortable in his own excrement—that would be considered abuse or, at the very least, negligence.

In the 1930s, Dr. Benjamin Spock advocated for very early infant training. He renounced this some years later subsequent to observing babies who regressed at 15 and 18 months after having been trained early on, often resulting in a mother-child conflict that lasted until the child was three or four years old. Dr. Spock surveyed other mothers who procrastinated potty training; these children eventually decided to use the toilet on their own and gained control over their bladder and bowel movements simultaneously.

Thomas Berry Brazelton (2004), a paediatrician from Cambridge, Massachusetts, promoted self-training in 1,500 consecutive patients, ages two-and-a-quarter and two-and-three-quarters. He instructed parents to allow their children to decide when it was time to start using the toilet, promoting the natural evolution of the learning process. Very few of these children had later issues with chronic bedwetting. The American Academy of Paediatrics (AAP) adopted Dr. Brazelton's recommendations in the 1990s, supporting child-oriented training—at the child's pace per behavioural cues. The AAP suggests children be amid 24 and 48 months before starting potty teaching.

"I don't have to wipe; my pee will wash it away."
Talen, age 2¾

It is true that when a child is ready to graduate from diapers, he needs to learn the proper hygiene rituals that go along with using the toilet—wiping front to back for girls, aiming into the toilet for boys, thoroughly washing the hands—so some instruction from the parent is necessary. If a child wants to cooperate but lacks the coordination essential to do so, we may be inadvertently setting him up to fail. The child may present as willing to learn but may have difficulty with the mechanics that enable successful toileting experiences. As parents, we need to equip our children with the necessary resources that will ensure victory over this course of development. If climbing up on the toilet is too daunting or physically challenging for your child, then provide a potty that sits on the floor. If manipulating the toilet paper roll is problematic, causing a mound of product to cascade along the floor to gather dust bunnies, then give your child a box of tissue instead. Placing child-sized benches in the bathroom makes it easier to reach the soap dispenser and sink, helping to promote hand washing. Make sure clothing can be easily pulled up and down. Zippers and buttons are difficult for little hands to manipulate and become even more awkward when the child is bouncing around doing a pee dance out of urgency.

"Vanesa, why don't you stay out and play with the kids?"
"Be-why I peed my pants."
Auntie, age 20-something
Vanesa, age 2½

When our eldest was in junior kindergarten, I sent him to school one day wearing the cutest pair of overalls. I received a call midmorning from the teacher, informing me that he had had an accident. She requested I bring him a change of clothes. As I approached the school, I could feel his humiliation hot on my cheeks and felt the urge to scoop him up in my arms and comfort him. I stood outside the JK room until the teacher caught my eye and quietly sent my son out to meet me. I smiled at him, communicating my understanding, and we went into the staff bathroom, where I cleaned him up and changed his clothes. I kissed him on the cheek where a tear had been, then watched him slip back among his peers unnoticed. We didn't say a word to each other that day. We didn't need to. I recognized how difficult it was for him to undo the clasps on those overalls; he knew I understood.

I, unfortunately, have personal insight into such embarrassment and remember all too vividly how I felt in a similar situation. In the late 1980s, after returning home from partying at a university pub, I was having great difficulty getting my mini jean skirt to go down over my hips. I really had to go and was in the midst of quite a pee dance when my roommate offered to help me out. The two of us pulled and tugged on my skirt but it just wouldn't go down over my hips. We were laughing so hard that I fell on top of her and proceeded to get us both wet.

Regrettably, that was not the first time this roommate fell prey to one of my bladder calamities. There was another such occurrence when sunbathing in a small motorboat in the middle of a lake. When it came time for us to return to shore, my friend began pulling on the starter cord to get the motor running. It was a finicky process and usually required a few hard tugs to get it going. I was lying at the bow of the boat when one vigorous pull disengaged the cord from the motor, causing my friend to fall back and land on top of me. Immobilized by hysterical laughter, I lost control of my bladder once again, getting us both wet. It's not surprising we went our separate ways after graduation.

I am shamefully notorious for having wet my pants on more than a just a few occasions. Another time, when pregnant, I sneezed in a video rental store and stood in horror as a warm stream ran down the length of my leg and gathered in a pool at my feet—I was wearing white!

> *"Yeah, Grandma, yeah, you went*
> *pee on the potty! Good girl!"*
> Vanesa, age 2½

When I'm not having accidents that are a result of poor clothing choices or gut-wrenching laughter, I actually have quite a shy bladder. I have a hard time going in a public washroom if a stranger is in the stall next to me. Try as I might, I have great difficulty going until that person has left the bathroom, which usually means I need a lot more time than the average intermission allows. As much as my husband thinks this is ludicrous, I could never imagine him promising me a candy treat if I managed a successful attempt when another person was in the adjacent cubicle. The only incentive for using the bathroom should be the relief in having taken care of your bodily needs—without the consequence of wetting or soiling yourself.

Society has bought into this notion of extrinsically motivating good behaviour, because initial results are usually quite favourable. At first, rewards work well in getting children to do something they typically refuse to do. Immediate results validate the use of behaviour modification and reinforce parents to keep rewarding. But the effects of these behavioural changes are often temporary. Children quickly adapt to the gimmee-gimmee-get philosophy so many parents employ. Two problems emerge from this: First, the child gets bored with the offered prize and ups the ante—wanting more pay for less work. Secondly, we condition children to expect praise or receive a prize for performance, and when they have not been able to achieve at the parents' level of expectation and a reward is not given, the child feels imperfect and inadequate. The long-term impact these feelings have on a child's self-esteem can be detrimental to his overall well-being. What we parents fail to recognize is that the use of candy treats, star stickers and awarded privileges does not make children feel valued; it is a measure in controlling their behaviour. It gives the message that we are not interested in how the child feels; we only care about his compliance and that there is little room for making mistakes. When the ramifications of these tactics begin to manifest themselves in misbehaviour and defiance (often in areas unrelated to toileting: sleep disturbance, temper tantrums, eating disorder), we neglect to associate it with the use of rewards.

Children need to know the correct reasons for using the toilet and not be pressured by the allure of a coveted prize. The only reward a child should expect for having learned to use the potty is an intrinsic satisfaction in achieving a developmental milestone.

"Did you hear that burp from my bum?"
Vanesa, age 2½

Worse than a temperamental bladder, I have a pathological bowel. I can only have a bowel movement in three places: my house, my mother's (because that is where I learned to use the toilet in the first place) and the cottage. I have gone away for a week at a time on business and felt as though I was going to explode by the time I got home. And my bowel knows when home is near. It begins to percolate just as I round the corner to the street that we live on. I have had too many close calls running up the stairs than I care to remember. And for those weeks when I am away from home, by the third or fourth day, I am usually plagued with stomach cramps and uncontrollable flatulence—none of which contribute to having a good time.

Realizing that these intricacies are not within the normal realm of experience for most people, sharing them will hopefully provoke thoughtful contemplation about the child's point of view when learning to use the toilet. I want to infuse an appreciation for the angst a child must feel when he cannot perform on demand, or has an accident. Laugh as we might over the absurdity of each of my legendary tales, they are not necessarily feel-good stories. I learned to use the toilet a very long time ago. Controlling and preventing such misfortunate events should be well within my scope of capabilities. No one has ever had the audacity to reprimand me for having had an accident or to shame me by suggesting I wear Depends undergarments; I've never been told I'm a bad girl, spanked or sent to my room without privileges for not having been able to go to the bathroom on demand. People have responded to me with humour and understanding: they have acknowledged my embarrassment and felt sorry for me (they may have thought there was something seriously wrong with me, too, but they never said it to my face). Paradoxically we treat our children, who are just learning the toileting process, with less empathy and respect than we would demand for ourselves.

In 1994, there was an article that appeared in *In Your Health* magazine entitled *The Potty Wars*, referencing toilet training accidents as the leading cause of serious abuse against children over the age of 12 months. Every interaction we have with our offspring should be an exercise in preserving their integrity. Children deserve to learn within a nurturing, respectful environment, cultivated by the parents' unconditional love and understanding. When the milieu is favourable, learning is less stressful for all those concerned.

> *"Talen, did you pee your pants?"*
> *"No! Kohan did when he was little, when these*
> *underwear belonged to him."*
> *Father, age 40-something*
> *Talen, age 3¾*

Children progress at a rate unique unto themselves; they will have accidents and will often regress in times of stress or change. Our middle child went through a period of regression that our first son did not experience. Both boys attended a home day care where the caregiver's husband passed away suddenly, and we needed to make other child-care arrangements for a period of two weeks. Our boys had been in this woman's supervision since our middle son was six months old, and they each had formed quite a bond with her during that year and a half. Not having the cognitive skills to comprehend death, our middle child was confused as to why he abruptly had to be watched throughout the day by someone else. He made quite a fuss during each of those mornings, but on the second day into the new routine, he emphatically told us, "My no poop in the potty until my go back to Dorfy's." The only explanation that made sense for why he was being so adamant was that he was trying to control the situation and force us into sending him back to his much-loved caregiver.

Our son began squatting behind the couch, prompting us to offer him a diaper, which he would sometimes accept, but not always. This went on every day until he returned to his babysitter's home, where he immediately resumed using the toilet. We felt it was necessary to respect how our child was feeling and allow him the opportunity to exercise what little control he thought he had over the situation. It was more important for him to feel secure than it was for us to have him continue using the toilet for his bowel movements. Not putting pressure on him communicated our regard and unconditional love for him, which was essential as he was working out feelings of perceived abandonment by his caregiver.

We were lucky in the sense that this child was so verbal and able to articulate his feelings and give warning as to what he was going to do. If this were not the case, it would have been up to us to clue into how he was feeling about the recent upset in his routine. As parents, we need to be sensitive to the changes and stresses in our children's lives that can have an undesirable impact on their behaviour. The birth of a sibling, moving to a new house, illness, or a parent gone away for a few days can negatively influence a child, causing him to regress to a previous level of development.

"See my pee in the toilet; isn't it beautiful?"
Talen, age 3

Our third son did not follow in the same path as his siblings did, with respect to learning to use the toilet. His induction into the world of no diapers was accelerated by the insistence of his eldest brother. He was two-and-a-half and really hadn't shown much interest in learning about the potty business. One morning while dressing to go off to day care, his eldest brother strongly encouraged him to try wearing "big boy" underwear, emphasizing that only babies wore diapers. This was not exactly the way I would have handled things, but I appreciated what our oldest boy was trying to do. Our youngest hated to be called a baby and took quite offence to the insinuation. Rising to the challenge, he put on a pair of underwear and told me he was going to day care as a "big boy." Having been cajoled into this daring act of going out in public without wearing a diaper, he surprisingly demonstrated great control over his bladder; he even managed to stay dry through the night. We were encouraged. However, his control over bowel movements was a completely different story—it was another seven months before he mastered competency in this task. Because he stubbornly rebuffed the use of disposables after that fateful morning with his older brother, we had to contend with cleaning up a lot of messes. It was a struggle between empowering his autonomy and doing what was convenient for us. This incredibly precocious boy thought only babies wore diapers. Knowing how he hated to be thought of as a baby, we couldn't in good conscience make him wear one—it was just too demeaning.

We began watching for a consistent time during the day when he would have an accident, or when he would hide under the dining room table, or when he appeared to be grimacing. During these notable precursors to having a bowel movement, we would encourage him to use the potty. Just mentioning that he should try to go on the toilet was enough to launch him into a fit of hysterical crying—clearly indicating that he wasn't emotionally ready. He had a really hard time giving up what he thought had been a part of who he was. After dumping the contents of his pants into the toilet in an attempt to show him where it preferably belonged, he would strongly object to flushing it down. He would even ask to keep it there until Daddy got home. I was a little freaked out; this preoccupation with one's bodily waste was a little weird to me and, truth be known, my patience was wearing thin, and I often reacted with frustration. In an effort to appease me I'm sure, he began highlighting his success with emptying his bladder in the toilet by jumping up and down, clapping his hands and stating how great he was for having used the potty. He also began holding the urge to have a bowel movement and became quite constipated with resultant tummy cramps. On the fourth day of one such episode, we had no other choice but to give him a glycerine suppository—something I would not recommend to anyone. He was so mad at me and was thoroughly convinced that I was purposely trying to hurt him. He went around for days telling his father and the day care staff that "Mommy hurt me by putting her finger in my bum." Honestly, it was not a proud parenting moment, trying to put that one into context.

We talked a lot after that about the importance of not holding in the urge to go even it meant having an accident. I would rather clean dirty pants than have my child get sick or become traumatized by giving him another suppository. Some weeks later, he began using the toilet more frequently, and accidents started to resemble their true definition and were no longer just measures of avoidance. Still reluctant to give away a part of him self, every flush necessitated a ceremonial bon voyage for several months following. He was three-and-a-quarter years of age when he finally used the toilet without dissension. It has now become a normal part of his daily activities of living, and his only reward for his accomplishment is relieving himself in a hygienic, socially acceptable way. According to him and his brothers, this achievement has transported him to the ranks of "big boy"—baby no more. And for this he is profoundly proud.

3

Fears

*"Don't cry, baby Catherine. A mommy is right
here—not your mommy, but she is a mommy."*
Talen, age 3½

During early infancy, anxiety is felt in response to physiological
stressors. The sensations that accompany hunger, elimination,
gastric upset and tiredness can be distressing for a newborn.
The parents' role during the first few months of development is
primarily focussed on relieving the child of these discomforts. If
the infant's needs are responded to in a sensitive, timely manner,
he learns to trust in the relationship he has with his caregiver
and, as a result, will discover how to manage his own anxiety.
As babies grow, there is a shift in the angst they feel resulting
from physiological needs to ones that are more psychological
in nature—like having to separate from their primary caregiver
and fearing the loss of love from a parent. Separation anxiety is
the first real manifestation of fear and usually peaks around 18
months of age. This is the time when most children engage in
playing games like peek-a-boo and hide and seek, where they
reinforce the guarantee that Mom and Dad will not disappear.

Temperament plays a major role in how well children are able to
deal with being separated from their parents. The character traits of
easy, difficult and slow to adapt predict the response an individual
child will have. Our *easy* eldest child welcomes the opportunity
for adventure and has never had a problem being away from us.
Rarely did he protest going to the babysitter—he usually reserved

that reaction for when it was time to go home. We once left him with his aunt and uncle for a few days when he was two-and-a-half, and he barely said goodbye to us because he was so excited to be staying with his cousins. A neighbour he didn't know all that well offered to watch him while his father and I went to visit his great-grandmother in hospital, and he scarcely noticed us leaving, as he was eager to play on the swing in her backyard. On his first day attending school, the teacher had to remind him to go back through the door and say goodbye to me and my husband, and he was oblivious to my standing there, crying.

> *"Mommy, you're not going away? You will sleep*
> *here? I will see you in the morning?"*
> *Talen, age 4*

It would be correct to assume that our other two sons were not so well adjusted when it came to separating from us. Our youngest child was a higher-needs baby, constantly requiring physical contact. When he was an infant, the only thing that seemed to work to get him to stop crying was if I literally strapped him to my body and wore him around like a shirt. Whoever invented those baby carriers has my utmost respect and admiration. My son absolutely loved it. When it was time for me to return to work, he did not do well at the sitters. His siblings were older than he was and already attending school so he was used to having Mommy all to himself during the day. He cried relentlessly. It was inconceivable to think his caregiver could give him her undivided attention. As wonderful as she was, it was impossible for her when she was looking after other children as well. Much to everyone's dismay, we had to take him out of that environment and look for alternative child care.

We hired a recent high school graduate to be our son's full-time nanny. She came into our home every weekday and provided him with the one-on-one attention he craved. This arrangement was a much better fit, given his higher-needs temperament. Our son and his nanny developed an enduring bond. She stayed with us for a year and half and then left to pursue other career opportunities. By this time, our baby was 24 months old so we considered, and decided upon, an organized day care facility. The transition was anxiety provoking for all of us. Most mornings after dropping him off, I would leave in tears as I could hear him wailing behind me. Typically he would settle down shortly after I left and engage in various activities without complaint—only to burst out crying the moment I came back for him; he was so relieved to see me. It took a month or so before he settled into the new routine. In the last three years, he has graduated twice to different levels of care. He currently attends the junior/senior kindergarten program and loves it. We still have mornings where he protests going—preferring to stay home with Mommy—but those days are few and far between. He continues to ask every day if I will be picking him up after work—still entrenched in the toddler notion that I will not come back, as if once out of sight, I magically disappear and cease to exist.

When he was 18 months, I went away on business for a week. When I returned home, he wouldn't even look at me and clung to his nanny for comfort. The next time I went away, this time for 10 days on a trip to Scotland with my sister, he was 21 months old. I made a video of myself reading his favourite stories, singing him songs he liked to hear and playing the piano. The nanny provided him with opportunities each day to watch it. When I got back this time, he welcomed me with open arms. (For the two older boys I made a scrapbook chronicling my would-be travels so they could follow me through my tour of Scotland each night as their father read it to them.) It's important to recognize that young children have no concept of time, so when we leave them, it can feel like forever.

"Mommy, no matter how big I get,
I will never outgrow you!"
                        Nolan, age 8½

Our second child's fear of separation didn't begin to manifest behaviourally until he was five or six years old, and it extends beyond the physicality of being away from us. He worries about my husband and me divorcing when we argue. He is concerned when we are angry with him, that we don't love him anymore. He often reports feeling like we don't care for him as much as we do his brothers; he doesn't feel like he fits into the family.

It's true, when you have three children, the eldest gets attention in terms of a lot of firsts, and the baby requires a lot of your time physically—often leaving the middle child vying for your attention. The middle child is imperviously stuck between the first pride and joy and the darling baby. When you're doing homework with the eldest and helping the youngest to toilet himself, the one in between needs to find things to do on his own to keep himself entertained. I can appreciate how he feels left out. We try and make it a point to spend a lot of one-on-one time with him—with the others too, but this middle son gets much more satisfaction out of these intimate moments with Mom and Dad than his brothers seem to. He needs to check in on his connection with us—it helps him re-establish his sense of belonging. His self-worth is contingent on how he perceives we feel about him. He internalizes a lot of what he thinks other people think about him. It has become a daily project for my husband and me to teach him about the value of how he sees himself and that what others think is less important. But for right now in these early years, we know that children develop a sense of well-being through the belief in the love their parents have for them. We tell each of our boys that we love them every night before they go to bed and every morning when they wake up. It is the first and last thing they hear, every day. When children feel loved, they are more secure in their surroundings and have less fear about being abandoned.

This need to feel loved and cared for does not fade away with age; it is an inherent need in all of us that lasts a lifetime. I found it interesting to hear my eldest sister say to me the other day that she loves to go blueberry picking with our parents because it's the one time she has them all to herself and she revels in it. I suppose that as we become children of aging parents, our childhood fear of separating from them resurfaces; only now, instead of worrying that they will magically disappear from our sight, we become afraid for when they will inevitably disappear from our lives.

> *"You're afraid of the dark!"*
> *"No, I'm not!"*
> *"Yes, you are! I can see a night-light right over there!"*
> *Cameron, age 8*
> *Keldan, age 9*

During the toddler years, our family experienced night terrors and nightmares as a natural developmental phenomenon. Each of our boys had difficulties of varying degrees with imaginary threats. As discussed in chapter 1, these sleep disturbances were resolved as we became more adept in assisting our children to use the strengths of their own personalities to defend against fear. By allowing them the opportunity to employ their own solutions to a problem, our children have grown more confident in their ability to manage and cope with phobia-induced anxiety. They have been empowered to try to work it out on their own, and they subsequently rely less and less on Mom and Dad to get rid of their fears for them. Our middle son insisted on sleeping on the top bunk—convinced that the monsters wouldn't be able to climb up after him. He therefore resolved his own fear through exercising control over the situation. Being a fabrication of his own making, these monsters he imagined didn't have arms, making the ascent up the bunk bed ladder impossible. He also thought that they had very small brains and therefore would never think to look for him up high near the ceiling—it made sense for him to sleep on the top bunk. We could have prevented him from trying out this hypothesis of his—it may have seemed illogical to us—but these monsters were a figment of his imagination, not ours, so it only stands to reason that he would be the one to know how to get rid of them. We supported his choice to move to the upper bed; he felt his contribution to solving his own problem was respected and valued. Our son gained confidence during this situation, and that's a powerful ingredient in the recipe for overcoming fears.

As the years pass, this child is less inclined to think there are monsters after him; however, he still doesn't like to sleep on the bottom bed and prefers to have a night-light on and his door left open. This little worrier of ours insists on knowing precisely where Mom and Dad are after he has gone to bed. He doesn't need us for anything in particular and manages quite well if we do happen to be somewhere other than the immediate vicinity, but it feels uncomfortable and takes him much longer to fall asleep.

I recently took the boys and stayed for the weekend at my parent's house. It was hot and humid, and they do not have air-conditioning so we decided to sleep in the basement, where it was cool. My mother made each of the boys a bed out of couch cushions on the floor, and I was set up in a small bedroom off the main recreation room. Our youngest son wasn't too happy about having to sleep on the ground ("with bugs") and was adamant about crawling into bed with Mommy. There are limitations sometimes to how far you can go to satisfy the needs of your children—it was hot, and I was sleeping in a single bed; it was not going to happen. He conceded to snuggling with me on the floor until he fell asleep, at which time I returned to my little room and read for a while. The middle child was feeling apprehensive about sleeping in the dark basement and insisted on leaving a small lamp on (for his younger brother, of course), and asked at least three times if I was going to remain in the basement with them (again, for the sake of his younger brother, who may wake up afraid and need me). Long after the youngest child was asleep, it was this middle son who got up half a dozen times to check that I was still in the room beside them. Silently he would peek around the door to see that I was still there, and then he would quickly return to his space on the floor. Each time, I pretended not to see him. His assurance in knowing I was nearby was enough to calm his fears about sleeping in the not-too-familiar basement of his grandparents' house. If I had made his presence known, he would have been embarrassed that I thought him afraid, and he would have resorted to acting out, as he typically did in these situations as a means of defending himself. Once convinced that I was not leaving them, he joined his two brothers in the land of slumber. How different these boys are; the eldest was asleep the moment his head hit the pillow, completely unaffected and totally unaware of the dangers these surroundings posed for his siblings.

As I looked at the three of them sleeping, I reflected on a time when I was living as a young adolescent in this house I grew up in. I had to go to the basement to get something from the laundry room. At the time, there was no light switch at the top of the stairs so you had to make your way down in the dark and feel along the length of the wall until you found the control to illuminate the rest of the way. Adjacent to the laundry room, there is a closet that hangs off-season coats, and storage boxes sit on an upper shelf. My sister had been pressing clothes that day, and, when finished, she had propped the ironing board against one half of the closet door, leaving the other half of the door ajar. On the way down the stairs, my eyes were adjusting to the lack of light, and I saw the ironing board, hanging coats and boxes in the closet as a giant ominous figure. I ran screaming like a lunatic all the way back up the stairs. I realized immediately that my eyes had played a trick on me, but intellectualizing what I had seen did nothing to eradicate the future need to always make sure the closet door was shut and the ironing board put away. And, on this night, before I slept in the basement with my children, I made sure the closet door was closed.

*"Mommy, please don't make me wear this vest on
my first day of school; it makes me feel so nervous."*
Nolan, age 6

Imaginary threats usually accompany earlier developmental stages and are self-limiting in nature. As children grow, they learn to distinguish between what is real and what is fantasy. School-aged children tend to worry more about universal issues like war, pollution and extreme weather; they will often fret over personal concerns as well, such as being afraid of failing school, rejection from peers or losing a loved one. Fears that are rooted in reality are more challenging to deal with and are not always overcome by rational thought. Those that have been confirmed by trauma may never completely go away; for example, a child may have a fear of earthquakes and then may actually be involved in one. Distress of this magnitude can have life-lasting consequences.

I have a friend who is petrified of flying. As I was preparing to write this chapter, I met her for coffee and asked if she knew where her fear of flying came from. During her senior year in high school, a plane leaving her hometown crashed because the wings had not been de-iced prior to takeoff. There were no survivors. While conveying this tragic story, I observed a noticeable change to her usual spirited demeanour. Her confidence appeared shaken. Tearfully she reminisced about a young family she babysat for who all lost their lives that day. I couldn't help but feel my own throat constrict and my eyes sting, forewarning tears. She explained that there wasn't a person in town who didn't know someone who was killed in that crash. It was a community catastrophe.

The pain of the memory reflected in her eyes was so apparent, and, for the first time since knowing her, I understood why she is so afraid to fly. Her fear of flying has always been a subject of humorous entertainment, and I realize now that all the joking and making fun of herself is a way of coping. She was laughing, telling me about a time when she took the advice of someone who suggested getting drunk while on a plane. Drinking herself into oblivion sounded like a good idea, but in actuality she spent the duration of the flight huddled under a blanket with only her eyes peering out in a paranoid gesture, inciting the flight attendant to ask if she was all right. Alcohol is a depressant so its consumption only made the trip more unbearable for her. This friend of mine is a rational, intelligent, incredibly strong woman, so I was saddened as I listened to her chastise herself for not being able to overcome her fear. Attempts in therapy to gain control over the terror she feels when flying have not proved that successful. When work necessitates travel by air, she takes essential measures against having a panic attack by asking her physician to write a prescription for a benzodiazepine. Heavily medicated is the only way she can manage to fly.

In response to my inquiry about what flying feels like for her, she answered, "Utterly alone, vulnerable."

> *"If I go swimming in the lake and you let go of*
> *me, the sharks will come and eat me."*
> *Kohan, age 5*

Every year, my husband and I take the boys to a pumpkin patch on the Saturday prior to Halloween. It's not your typical plot of land where the only excitement is a spirited race through a muddy field in search of the finest orange-skinned piece of fruit for carving. The pumpkin patch we go to hosts a myriad of activities: pony rides, juggling clowns, a corn maze, a magic show, tractor rides and two haunted barns. One barn is for children six to twelve years of age, and the other is for anyone over the age of sixteen who is brave enough to enter. I don't have the enthusiasm or the courage to tour the adult haunted barn. The TV show "House of Frankenstein" was frightful enough for me as a young girl, and I have never really recovered from the traumatic experience of seeing the film *Amityville Horror* when I was a teenager. I don't advocate frightening yourself as a choice of entertainment and admit to having little understanding of people who do. Adults can make their own decisions about purposely frightening themselves, but I believe it is the parents' responsibility to protect the innocence of their young.

On one occasion while visiting the pumpkin patch, we had stopped outside the petting zoo to feed a couple of goats when we heard a deafening scream. We quickly turned around to identify the source of commotion and saw a young boy being forced by his mother through the door of the kid's haunted barn. Undersized, fighting his mother, he made futile attempts at biting and kicking to get her to release him. The mother was shouting over his protests, "Look, nobody else is crying. Everyone is having fun. Stop being such a suck." This determined mother had little tolerance for her son's unwillingness to go into the barn. Goading him into submission only proved counterproductive; the name-calling made him more resistant and defiant. It was so obvious how terrified that little guy was. It was obvious to everyone except his mother.

How I wish that mother would have stopped long enough to allow the moment to reveal itself so she would hear her son's voiced remonstration and see the fear manifested in his body movements. If she would have taken the time to appreciate the situation from her child's point of view and put herself in her son's experience and remember what it was like to be young and afraid, I am certain she never would have forced him through those haunted corridors. She would have made a different choice—a choice that would have preserved that child's need to rely on his mother's understanding and unconditional regard for who he was.

> *"Mommy, you know I don't like thunder! Oh, I can't live this night."*
>
> *Nolan, age 8½*

Last summer, while vacationing at the cottage, a violent storm ripped through in a very short period of time, causing an incredible amount of damage. The morning had been bright with sunshine, and we had spent it lazing around the beach. A faint breeze could be felt off the lake, but it was warm and calm. There wasn't a cloud in the immediate sky. It was not the type of weather that forebodes a torrential downpour, and we had no idea the conditions would change so drastically, so fast. Shortly after lunch, I was rocking our youngest on the family swing, enticing him to have a nap, when my husband called out to me, bringing my attention to a portentous dark cloud looming overhead. I had no sooner gotten up off the swing and laid our child down in the cottage when it became black as night outside and hail began to plummet down on the roof, sounding like an avalanche. A funnel cloud could be seen hovering over the lake, and lightning tore through the sky. Trees that had been on the property for as long as I can remember were uprooted by the forceful wind, causing them to take out power lines, resulting in cottages with interiors that matched the opaque scene outside. The enormous trunks of the uprooted trees splintered over the acreage. The canopy on the deck was torn to shreds and its storm-mangled aluminium frame was strewn all over the side lawn. Our children's 12-foot trampoline flew through the air at 30 feet, smashing into the side of the neighbour's cottage and destroying their eaves trough. My husband and I were hysterically running around outside, trying to fasten down anything we could manage to get our hands on. I moved vehicles out of harm's way, from falling trees, and my husband strapped down the trampoline so it could not cause any further damage. From inside the cottage, our two older sons watched in horror through the picture window. At the time, we were not consciously aware of the boys' pleadings for us to come in. In retrospect, I remember hearing them calling out for us, their voices stricken with fear.

The 20 minutes it took for this tornado-like storm to reap havoc on our surroundings pales in comparison to the impairment it has caused our middle son. Having a more anxious personality than our older boy, and being that much younger at the time of witnessing the power of nature's fury, he has been significantly impacted. Weather has become a persistent concern for him. He is preoccupied with watching the weather channel and constantly asks his father what the weather report is for tomorrow. Knowledge can be helpful in most circumstances, but when you're only eight years old, it can be hazardous when partnered with an overactive imagination. A storm in another part of the country sends him reeling, as he thinks about how it will affect the people living there. Any amount of rain or wind has him taking cover in the basement, sobbing under blankets.

We are working to empower him to confront this fear. We attempt to ground his imagination with rational thought by encouraging him to evaluate the force of a current storm by asking himself questions: Are people still able to walk on the sidewalks or drive their cars on the streets? Is rain or snow breaking the windows or penetrating the walls of our home? Are objects larger than a stop sign being hurled through the air? The answers he gives himself help to put the degree of each storm's severity into perspective. My husband is particularly good at getting our son to evaluate and put a current experience into context because my husband remembers vividly as a boy how preoccupied he was with thoughts of war. Every plane that flew overhead or crack of thunder he heard translated in his mind to a bomb exploding. He identifies with our son's fearful ideas much better than I do, and he finds interesting and creative ways to get our son to critically analyse the weather. They spend time watching what direction the wind is blowing the clouds, what colour the sky is and how many stars are out at night. They look to see if cows are lying down or if mosquitoes are rampant because all of these things can be an indication as to whether or not it will rain. My husband is also the master of analogies. He has described for our son that the worry part of our son's brain is very small, but it smoulders like a fire, and that the thoughts he has are like wood, which add fuel to this fire, making it bigger. He says the thinking part of our son's brain is like water, and when he thinks realistically about the threat the weather poses, he douses the worry fire brain with water, putting it out. Our son incorporates these analogies into his repertoire of coping skills and makes moderate use of them. The long-term goal is to have him reverse the negative thinking and minimize the fear he feels as much as possible.

Although the weather makes him anxious, it has not prevented him from leaving the house or attending school. He admits to feeling nervous outside the home if a storm is going on, but he successfully contains his emotions. How he is able to restrain himself, I am not entirely sure. He says it's because he does not want his friends to laugh at him; nonetheless, it speaks to his strength of character in maintaining control. My husband and I work with his strengths, highlighting the potential for them to overcome his fear. For these reasons, we continue to tackle this issue in the absence of professional intervention. Should this become a pervasive crisis, where it inhibits his ability to play or go to school, we will need to employ outside help.

This is where knowing your child's personality type is so vital to successful parenting, and trial and error is pivotal. We have discovered that diversion works well in this situation. Once when it started to rain, and predictably our son began to panic, my husband involved him in building some new steps for the deck. This child aspires to be a structural engineer and takes great pleasure in building things. They were outside sheltered under a canopy, cutting wood when it really began to pour. Instead of concentrating on the rain, our son continued with the task at hand. I commented on how brave he was to be working outside in the rain. He looked around a bit amazed himself, shrugged his shoulders and gave me the biggest smile. Only just a few days ago, during a thunderstorm, my sister got him to focus on the positive consequences of rain—it feeds the earth so trees and crops can grow, keeps the lakes from drying up—this change in attitude toward the weather had quite a calming effect. (Unfortunately, this only works when you can convince him to divert his attention; that in itself sometimes takes longer than the storm lasts.) I now insist that he tells me positive things about the weather. He needs to replace every worry thought with a more realistic notion. When he is able to rewire his thinking in a positive direction, I can visibly see the anxiety diminish.

Our second-born is a highly sensitive, worrisome, deep-thinking child. The positive to all that is that he loves fiercely, empathizes with others' pain and is incredibly generous. He is also the most tenacious of our boys; it may take him longer to try something new, but once he starts, he never gives up. He is the one who will ski a double black diamond, climb to the top of a rock-climbing wall, or try somersaults on the trampoline—but only when he understands the mechanics of such endeavours and has assessed the risk involved. He is extremely conscientious. These are noble character traits, especially in someone so young. We are not interested in changing anything about him; our only goal is in helping him to manage better. His personality requires constant reassurance and infinite descriptions of detail. This inquisitive boy asks as many questions about a situation as his racing thoughts will allow, until he is satisfied he has every aspect worked out in his mind. When change is unavoidable, we need to explain with the same intensity and velocity as we did the original plan. He hates surprises; surprises are threatening to him. He is distrustful of the unknown, always concerned that what he doesn't know will result in catastrophe. Knowing this about him makes it much easier to be proactive. We simply give him the necessary details he requires, at a level that is appropriate for his developmental stage. When we do not answer his questions to his satisfaction, he becomes quite overwhelmed with curiosity and demands information, often regressing into tantrums. It can be exhausting, having to answer so many questions about the same thing, over and over again. But the alternative is watching him torture himself with his fear of the unknown. I heard a guest speaker at a spiritual retreat once say, "A mother is only as happy as her saddest child." I believe that to be true.

One Christmas, we decided to surprise the boys and take

them to Florida. They got up on Christmas morning, totally unassuming, opened their stockings and gifts from Santa and then, an hour before departure, we announced the family trip. It seemed like a great idea at the time, to keep it a secret until the last moment. Knowing what we know about how our one son reacts to surprises, I am bewildered at our own stupidity. As expected, our second child was not enthusiastic about this impromptu change in plans. With a pensive look on his face, he began asking questions: "Florida is in the United States; I don't know anybody in the United States except for an uncle in Chicago. Is Florida close to Chicago? Isn't the United States at war? How are we going to get there? How long is it going to take? Where are we going to stay? What does the condo look like? What are we going to do in Florida? So we won't be seeing Grandma and Grandpa? What about our cousins—will we see them? Well, when will we see them? What about Toby (the dog)? Who will look after her? When will we be back?"

It wasn't the trip to Florida that was disappointing for our son; it was the fact that he had it all straight in his mind for weeks, what his Christmas vacation was going to look like. He had no idea what this new plan entailed. He may have also felt a sense of betrayal because his concrete way of thinking would perceive this abrupt change as having been lied to. Essentially, we did lie to him. There was not much we could do in this situation but address his fear of the unknown by answering his questions with patience and understanding. Once he was able to conceive a picture in his mind of what to expect, the anxiety diminished, and he began to relax and enjoy the adventure—at least until the next day when his incessant inquiries began all over again: "What are we doing today? What is there to do there? How long does it take to get there? How much does it cost to go there? How long will we stay? Will we have lunch there? What will I have to eat? Will we have time to swim at the pool when we get back? What time will I have to go to bed?"

When we oblige this part of our child's personality by attuning to his need for reassurance in the form of information, we help him to combat the anxiety he feels. It's like putting the pieces of a puzzle together until a clear picture emerges, and an appreciation for its image is realized.

It was a memorable trip for all of us, but I think, out of the three of them, he had the most fun. He learned to use a skim board at the beach, he went rock climbing and bungee jumping on a trampoline, rode his first roller coaster and danced on New Year's Eve with his mother in a room full of people, like nobody was watching.

4
Eating

"You be the baby pony, and I'll be the mother
pony, and I will breast-feed you."
"Okay, but don't take your shirt off this time!"
Ava, age 3
Friend, age 4½

While sitting in my obstetrician's office at my six-week checkup after the birth of our first child, my son began to fuss in my arms, which I recognized as his cue that it was time to be fed. I had no qualms about breast-feeding in public, except that this child was very vocal when he ate, making my effort in being discreet next to impossible. As soon as he would latch on, he would begin to hum a tune of innocent pleasure that ranged from satisfaction to ecstasy. He was particularly noisy during this feeding, and a fellow patient made a comment likening my breast milk to liquid gold. Well, it was apparent that my son certainly thought it was.

I breast-fed on demand because it seemed like the most natural thing to do. As an adult, I'm not always hungry at the same time every day; it varies with how much I have had for breakfast or if a midmorning snack pushes lunch into the later afternoon, consequently delaying supper. I don't always eat the same amount at every meal either. There are days when I am ravenous and others when I hardly feel like eating at all. I can't reference the hunger pangs of another human and don't expect that someone could testify to the specifics of my appetite. Predicting when our child needed to be fed was distressing to us.

We couldn't justify putting our child on a strict feeding schedule because it didn't fit with our parenting philosophy of attuning to the needs of our children. We knew we wouldn't deny a hungry baby just because according to the schedule it wasn't time to feed him yet. We allowed our children to tell us when they wanted to eat and subsequently when they had had enough.

When our babies fussed or cried, causing my breasts to tingle, fill and let down, releasing that elixir of life, we knew it was time to feed. When they pulled away from my breast, making a popping sound so distinctive of a suction cup letting go, we knew they were done. My husband would take them from me to burp, giving me a chance to get my garments back in order, stretch my legs and perhaps do something else. My boy's father took a very active role in the pre and post work of breast-feeding each of them. Bottle-feeding is not the only way to get Dad involved. My husband would get up in the middle of the night, change the diaper and bring the infant to our bed, where we would lie and nurse. Once we were finished, my spouse would take the baby and put him back in his crib (if we didn't all fall back to sleep and stay there till morning). It was a team effort. I certainly felt supported, and our sons were nurtured by both their parents.

Providing sustenance from my own body to another human being and having it received with such pleasure was the most gratifying experience I have ever had. It never occurred to me to feed my newborns any other way—and not because I'm a tree-hugging, granola-eating mother who believes "breast is best." It was a practical decision. Breast-feeding was so convenient and economical. The human female body keeps milk at the exact temperature the baby needs, adjusting to the weather. It produces milk relative to the baby's demand. As the baby grows and his intake requirements increase, and then decrease after solid foods are introduced, the mammary glands produce enough milk accordingly. Breast-feeding could happen any time, anywhere: when pulled over on the side of the highway because home was too far away and a screaming infant has no regard for the concentration required to drive; walking through the mall during the Christmas holidays when the crowds were thick, and getting to a place where I could sit down was like breaking out of Alcatraz; at the beach where there wasn't a microwave or kettle to boil water for miles; and, most interestingly, during a wedding ceremony, in a strapless dress. I was lucky, though, because breast-feeding came so easy to me and to all three of my boys.

In contrast, my best friend's experience with nursing her first child was painful in every aspect from cracked nipples to mastitis to her daughter being what we called a "lazy sucker", only taking in the first surge of milk and not wanting to work for the important hind milk that makes babies fat. Her child was barely gaining the necessary weight at each checkup. Her paediatrician encouraged her to persevere with breast-feeding, disallowing the need to supplement with formula, making my friend feel like she had no other choice but to stay the course. This exhausted mother endured weeks of feeding her infant through a tube attached to her nipple and wrapped around the end of her finger, which she inserted into the baby's mouth. When she wasn't physically feeding her child, she was attached to an electric pump trying to keep her milk production up. She would journal the details of every feeding session, estimating her child's intake and monitoring output. It was such a mechanical endeavour; there was no joy in the experience. She was frustrated, depleted of energy and wished to be doing something else—anything to escape the confines of the entrenched beliefs of perfect Motherhood. She began to self-reproach, chastising herself for failing. Watching her go through such anguish was heartbreaking, and I was worried that she was becoming depressed. I single-handedly executed an intervention where I sat with her and told her enough was enough. She tells me now that I was the only one to give her permission to bottle-feed. *Permission!* Like she needed authorization to do what was in the best interest of her and her child.

*"Grandma, you breast-fed Uncle Alex and
Momma; did you breast-feed Grandpa too?"*
Ava, age 3

Although I agree there are many advantages to breast-feeding over bottle-feeding, I also understand that, in some instances, it is not the best choice for Mom or babe. Sometimes it just doesn't work out, making bottle-feeding necessary. That doesn't mean bottle-feeding has to be the default choice with subsequent children; my friend had a wonderful breast-feeding experience with her second child—but, then again, he was a completely different baby from her first. I encourage every mother to try nursing her baby, but at the same time I advocate feeding an infant in a way that will be mutually beneficial. It is important to choose the method that will cause the least amount of stress for Mom and babe. If breast-feeding is nerve-racking for Mom (attributable to any number of reasons), and the baby feels his mother's anxiety and becomes frustrated, it may be detrimental to the mother-infant relationship.

Dr. Sears believes that when a mother chooses to breast-feed, she continues with the oneness that she and her baby experienced during pregnancy. The woman's body continues to provide nourishment, warmth, comfort and safety, just as it did when the baby was in uteri. Dr. Sears says that the closeness shared during the breast-feeding experience allows the mother and child to tap in to one another's personality, and this shared oneness is thought to affect how the parent and child relate and communicate with one another for years to come. I agree that breast-feeding probably promotes more frequent interactions between Mom and babe because breast milk digests quicker than formula, necessitating that breast-fed babies eat more often. However, when breast-feeding is not an option, a mother *can* create other moments outside of feeding where she connects with and gets to know her child, ensuring attachment to one another.

Anecdotally, I was the only child my mother breast-fed. It

wasn't fashionable when my older sisters were born. To see the four of us together, you would not be able to discern which one of us she breast-fed in terms of the bond she shares with each of us. Our mother loves us independently, admires our individuality and has a connection unique to each of us in relation to who she is. We were all hugged and kissed often, loved greatly and listened to always. Her attachment to us is diverse but equal in depth and durability. There is no difference between my relationship with my mother and the relationships she has with my bottle-fed siblings.

> *"If you won't let me have a cookie before*
> *breakfast, how am I going to grow any bigger?"*
> Talen, age 4

We began introducing solid foods in the form of barley cereal to our first-born when he was four months old—mostly because a well-meaning neighbour commented that he was a small baby and probably wasn't getting enough to eat. What did I know? This was my first child, and she had four. Within two weeks, we discovered that we had made a mistake. Our child's digestive system was not quite ready, and he became terribly constipated. Our happy, contented baby turned miserable. We abruptly stopped feeding him solid food and waited until he was six months before starting again. At this time, he adjusted well, and, with the same vocal intensity in which he breast-fed, he shrieked with delight as he gobbled up his cereals, fruits and veggies.

We made the choice to make our own baby food—again for practical reasons—it was more economical. It was also important to us that we had control over what additives and nutrients we were giving our child. Making our own food from fresh fruits, meats and vegetables ensured that there were no chemical additives, preservatives or pesticides. It was not as time-consuming as one might think. We would simply add an extra pot to our stove when we were making dinner. When the contents were cooked, we puréed them in a food processor and poured them into ice cube trays to freeze. We could make several meals at a time this way, combining different foods, herbs and spices, giving variety to our sons' diets. The food processor allowed us to increase the consistency of the food on an incremental basis. It went from being puréed to mash to chunks, until our children ate the same meals as we did. In comparison to many of our friends who chose to feed their children ready-made baby food, our boys seemed to eat from the table much earlier, making mealtime more of a family affair, with everyone gathering at the same time and eating the same foods.

When our boys were learning to eat within a social setting, we spent most of the meal instructing them not to throw their food, sippy cups or spoons. We repeatedly handed them back the item they had chucked, asking them to pass it to Mommy if they were all done and reiterating "please" and "thank you." Often, we had to remove everything from their trays so they understood that throwing food and dinnerware was not acceptable. Then we had to endure hearing them wail in protest. The more we responded in this matter-of-fact way, the less inclined they were to throw things. We encouraged them to feed themselves as much as possible, fostering independence and table manners. They were given safe utensils as soon as they could grasp objects. By watching how we manipulated such paraphernalia, they learned to use them properly. I am confident when they are elsewhere for dinner that they are well-behaved and rehearsed in mealtime etiquette.

> *"Lord, I love you, Lord, you're great. I pray for my food and you appreciate. Oh yes, oh yes. What would I do without you, without you, without you? Amen."*
> *Nolan, age 7*

There is no better way to model table manners and create family unity than eating together on a daily basis. From the time our children could speak, dinner has been a time when we come together to discuss what were the best and worst parts of everyone's day. You learn a lot about what's going on with your children when you engage in active discussion at the table. It's a convenient place because everyone is in attendance and facing one another. My husband and I subscribe to the old adage: *the family that eats together stays together.* This belief has long been entrenched in my family of origin, and I can remember many nights sitting at the dinner table well into the late evening, talking to my parents. The food was all gone, and the milk got warm, but the conversation was unending. Our children have come to know that you do not leave the table until everyone is finished eating—or, more importantly, finished talking. Every time one of them would get up from the table before the meal was done (as they often do when they transition from high chair to sitting at the table), he was gently guided back to his seat and informed of the importance of staying until everyone agreed to be dismissed. That wasn't always easy, and we spent a lot of meals running around after rambunctious children. But, in all things you do consistently, a habit is formed. The boys have come to appreciate this family time and love when friends and relatives come over and join in our ritual. After giving thanks for the food that we are so blessed to be eating, our youngest usually starts things off by announcing the best "party" of his day.

> *"Vicki, eat your supper; do you know there are*
> *children starving in the world?"*
> *"You can send them my food, Daddy."*
> Father, age 40-something
> Vicki, age 5

Mealtime does not always resemble an episode from "Leave It to Beaver." As the boys get older, we hear numerous complaints about what's for dinner and petitions to make something different. Many nights, I sit down at the table bracing myself against some critical comment about the smell or appearance of what has been prepared. I can't figure out what happened. A metamorphosis took place with each of them around the age of three where we could no longer get our eldest to eat cooked vegetables, or our middle child to eat anything but pizza or spaghetti without complaint or our youngest to eat eggs. They all had the same rate of exposure to a wide variety of foods and ate them willingly for a significant period of time. When our eldest son was a toddler, he would eat lima beans by the handful for an afternoon snack. You couldn't get him to eat a lima bean now if it was the last food on earth. When I question them about the drastic changes in their appetites, they basically tell me that it's no big deal—they just don't like certain foods anymore.

If we gave into every complaint, we would spend hours trying to meet the requests of each family member. We've had to instil rules in our house that help buffer this type of mealtime pandemonium. My husband and I make it explicitly clear that we do not run a restaurant. We will only make concessions on those things that do not need extra preparation or are truly not tolerated. For instance, our eldest will not eat cooked veggies, but he will eat them raw so we provide cut peppers, carrots, cucumbers and the like for his consumption. I'm perfectly okay with this because you leave most of the nutrients behind in the boiled water of cooked vegetables anyway. Our middle child hates fish. Salmon is a favourite among the rest of us, which makes for an unpleasant scenario if we do not substitute his meal. The first time he tried fish as a toddler, he gagged at its repugnant odour and texture. We have tried to reintroduce it into his diet over the years, but he responds in the same manner in which he did the first time he tasted it. Consequently, we have something else on hand for him when we eat fish.

I have discovered over the last few years that sometimes it's the presentation and delivery of the food that makes all the difference to children. Our son who refuses to eat cooked vegetables loves homemade turkey and chicken soup—rich in carrots, zucchini, tomatoes and lentils. He also enjoys chili full of chickpeas, kidney beans and black-eyed peas. The youngest will eat cold egg salad sandwiches cut with cookie cutters. Sometimes our family dinners are served on good china, and we light candles and drink milk out of fancy wine glasses. We've done the opposite to elegant dining as well, where we spread out a blanket in the middle of the living room and have had indoor picnics. Once a month, sometimes twice, we have "whatever you want night" for supper. The boys love this because they can choose among their favourites and take an active role in preparing what they are going to eat. It's never really sophisticated, so prep and cleanup are not too cumbersome. The boys gain some autonomy around meal choices and get a break from having to eat what Mom and Dad always choose.

We haven't found better ways to offer our middle son fish—sometimes kids just truly hate certain foods, and when that's the case, we will not force our boys to eat it. My one sister strongly believes that you should not make a child eat something he does not like. She was a picky eater when she was young and remembers feeling like she had no choice about eating the foods she hated. Once, while visiting relatives, she became ill with a gastrointestinal flu. Our aunt had been cooking spaghetti at the time, and the farmhouse where my sister was staying reeked of stewed tomatoes and herbs. The smell of spaghetti sauce made my sister nauseated for years to come, and she refused to eat pasta for the longest time. My sister rejected a lot of foods when she was young. Her sandwiches always came home from school uneaten, squished and a little soggy. She hated cooked peas, and bananas were repulsive to her. She has resolved most of her dislikes as an adult and has become quite adventurous in the foods she is now willing to try, but the memory of having to sit at the table for hours to finish a meal has not been forgotten.

When parents insist that children eat food they detest or that they consume quantities larger than they have capacity for, children learn to ignore the signals of their own bodies. They become accustomed to having their feelings discounted and so they learn to rely on other people to tell them what their bodies need. The consequences of this can be quite detrimental to a child's well-being later on. As a teenager, he will be far more likely to succumb to peer pressure with regards to drugs and alcohol and sexual promiscuity than if his feelings regarding food were valued early on. Remember how the breast-fed baby pulls away from his latch, indicating he has had enough to eat? That baby knows instinctively to listen to his own belly telling him he is full. If we allow our children the freedom to pay attention to their body's internal messaging system, then they are more apt to make healthy choices concerning their own bodies.

Now having said that does not mean you allow your children to eat whatever they want, whenever they want. There needs to be balance in our diets. If we do offer foods that have little nutritional value, we make sure we do it in moderation. As a student nurse, I offered a seven-year-old patient some ginger ale after she had had a tonsillectomy. Her mother quickly intervened, telling me that her daughter had never had pop. We tried not giving our guys soft drinks—until they returned home from friends' birthday parties wearing Orange Crush moustaches. At any rate, pop is not a staple in our home so the boys do not ask for it except on special occasions. The same principle applies to dessert and sugar snacks. They don't get itemized on the grocery list and are therefore not available in our home on a regular basis. The majority of foods we offer are nutritionally sound, and there is enough variety for our children to glean the proper vitamins and proteins they require. One way to assess if you are providing healthy choices for your family is by evaluating where you buy most of your products from within the grocery store. If you spend more time picking things off the shelf in the middle aisles than from the periphery of the store where all the fresh produce and dairy is located, then perhaps you need to review your family's diet.

Children generally do not eat three square meals a day; in fact, six smaller meals per day are probably more accurate and suitable for growing children. So, when they're constantly asking for something to eat, I prefer it be an apple or a piece of cheese or yogurt than something chock-full of sugar that has no health benefit.

"I can't eat any more; my tummy is so angry with me."
Kohan, age 4

When our children insist they have had enough to eat, we respect that they know what their bodies are telling them. Can you imagine going out for dinner and not being able to finish your meal, and the maitre d' tells you that you cannot leave the restaurant until you have eaten everything you ordered? I would guess that you would be quite offended and not likely to return to that establishment ever again. When food is left uneaten, we wrap it up and place it in the fridge for the immediate future. When the boys inevitably come to us an hour later and tell us they are hungry, we simply heat up what they didn't eat at supper and serve it to them. It is only after they have finished what has been put on their plates that they can choose to have something else. This works particularly well when dessert or special treats are involved—like during Halloween. I have a brilliant friend who donates to the "Halloween Fairy." She takes all the candy she does not want her children to consume and leaves it out for the Halloween Fairy to take and replace with a toy. Her kids get to keep a few of their favourite treats, which only last a couple of weeks in her house, as compared to the month it takes us to get rid of ours. By that time, we are into Christmas, and Halloween treats are replaced with sugar cookies and candy canes. The boys have come to expect that when they have finished their supper, they may have a treat. But just because they expect this to happen doesn't mean they don't try and argue the point of getting what they want. We simply reiterate that when they have finished eating what is in front of them, and if they are still hungry, then they may have a treat.

> *"Talen, did you sneak a chocolate?"*
> *"No, Mommy. Toby ate one, and then she licked my face."*
> *Mother, age 30-something*
> *Talen, age 3½*

If we want our children to make healthy choices about food and prevent obesity and associated health risks, we need to model it for them. My sisters and I didn't grow up on junk food, and any sweets we did consume were baked fresh by my mother or grandmother. We ate pies rich in blueberries and raspberries picked from bushes in our backyards, and rhubarb from my grandpa's garden made into jam was delectable on tea biscuits. A treat on a Saturday night once in a blue moon consisted of popcorn and a small glass of ginger ale. Cola rarely made an appearance in our house unless my father put a shot of rum in it for his own enjoyment on a rare night when my parents were entertaining friends. Orange pop was about as daring as my parents got, and a case of 24 had to last me and my two sisters a whole summer. If we offered one to a friend, that meant we had one less for ourselves. I don't think it was because my parents were fastidious about nutrition—they are more inclined to be conscious about that now as they are aging. It was more economical to buy things out of necessity than to spend money on foods that were not good for you. Fast-food restaurants weren't as popular as they are today, and the investiture of ready-made dinners had not yet corrupted the wholesome family meal plan. My dad can't even pronounce "pizza," let alone eat one. Even so, my parents' eating habits were established by their parents. Once you're accustomed to eating organic fruits and vegetables, chemical-free meats and farm fresh dairy products, then processed foods are just not palatable to the diet. My husband's family came from a line of European farmers so he grew up eating the same kinds of foods I did. We, in turn, try to promote this kind of lifestyle to our children in hopes that the tradition of eating healthfully will continue with their generation and the next.

5

Sibling Rivalry and Conflict Resolution

"That baby takes up too much time."
"Yes. What do you think we should do about that?"
"Kill it!"

Caitlyn, age 4
Mother, age 30-something

A friend of mine was quite challenged by her four-year-old daughter when she brought home her second child from hospital. I was there one day when she was breast-feeding her newborn and her daughter requested to have a drink from the fridge. Both her father and I offered to get it for her but she insisted it be her mother. When she was told that Mommy was busy with the baby, she launched into a full-fledged tantrum. As time went on, it got to the point where this determined preschooler refused assistance from anyone other than her mother. It became virtually impossible for my friend to continue breast-feeding her son. The angst she felt and the tantrums her daughter would have during feeding times were all too cumbersome.

When my husband carried our second child into our home for the first time, I followed them, toting a large fruit basket that we had received as a gift while in hospital. That basket became my inspiration for dealing with the challenge of breast-feeding a new baby in the company of an older sibling. Every morning, my toddler and I would go around the house picking out his favourite books, games, toys, treats and a sippy cup filled with juice, and we would place them in the basket for the day. When it was time to feed the baby, I would ask our eldest son to get the "feeding basket" and come join us on the sofa. He would excitedly take the basket's handle into his chubby little hands, nestle in beside me and his brother and start rummaging through the contents until he found something of interest. Together we would read, colour, play *I Spy* or count Cheerios. He always had a drink and something to eat on hand so I never had to interrupt nursing to fulfill a demanding request. The basket worked splendidly. The older boy looked forward to this time we spent together, and when the baby heard us talking, he would effectively suck harder, communicating his enjoyment in the activity as well. It was a benefit to all of us. I was able to spend time with both my children, especially in light of the fact that my second child ate so frequently. The baby got to know his brother at the same time he was forging a bond with me, and our eldest child felt included.

But even beyond providing quality time for our family, the feeding basket gave way to so much more. The task of weaning our second-born was extremely difficult, and if it weren't for the family unity that the feeding basket created, he may never have learned to drink from anything other than my breast. When we began to wean, I foolishly insisted on having quiet and sent my older child away from us. I abandoned our time together with the basket for solitude. Unfortunately, no amount of silence helped to transition this baby from breast to bottle. I started feeling stressed, knowing that I would soon be returning to work. After several weeks of trying, I was at a loss as to what to do next. It was my mother who suggested inviting my eldest child back into the fold. The basket restored, the three of us sat on the couch, and when I began to read and my eldest son began to chatter, the baby enthusiastically drank from the bottle. It was absolutely remarkable.

We did other things to help our son adjust to his new role as big brother. We made every effort to include him where his new brother was concerned. My husband and I made sure to give dual diligence to our older son when company stopped by to see the baby. We would often highlight something he had recently done or ask him to invite visitors in to see his new room. He was coined Mommy's little helper, and a stool was placed beside the change table so he could climb up and assist with diaper duty. When it was bath time, our eldest child sat in the large tub beside the baby in his smaller bathtub and gave a hand at washing his brother's extremities. We invested in a double stroller so he could sit alongside his younger sibling on outings. And most importantly, my husband and I made sure to carve out some time during each day to solely interact with him, in the absence of his new baby brother. During those early years, we had very few issues with sibling jealousy. It was as harmonious as we had wished for it to be.

> *"I hated your little face from the first day*
> *I saw it in the cradle."*
> Uncle Kenny (to my father), age 8

We did all the same things with the second (and again with the first) when the third child came home. However, there were variables we couldn't control this time, making the change less smooth than the first time. There is more of an age gap between the second and third child than there is between the first two. Our middle child had had a few more years than his older brother to grow accustomed to being the baby of the family. The boys' temperaments are also so very different. The older one easily goes with the flow; the second boy tends to be apprehensive about new situations. Our eldest son was already attending school full-time. The second child attended kindergarten half-time, which allowed him to come home to me and the baby in the afternoon instead of going to the caregiver—a caregiver he was lovingly attached to. A routine upside down, our second-born felt relatively dismissed when his little brother arrived. It didn't help matters that our third child was quite colicky, demanding much of our time. One of us constantly had that babe in arms, either trying to soothe him or feed him.

The feeding basket was utilized, but with less effectiveness this time. Nursing was one of the rare instances when our third child was calm and quiet. It should have been the best occasion to spend some quality time with our middle child. However, I have regrettable memories of not being able to keep my eyes open when reading aloud to him and not being able to concentrate on anything he was saying to me. I would ask him to repeat himself to the point of making him frustrated. It's no wonder he got bored quickly with the contents of the feeding basket and would go off to find other ways to entertain himself. The rest of the time during those infant days was also less than ideal. It's understandable why our second child had difficulty accepting this new addition to the family. He must have heard "in a minute," "not just now" and "please be patient and wait" over a thousand ca-trillion times! He naturally responded with defiance, temper tantrums and fits of crying.

The summer of my maternity leave, we went up to the cottage, and I spent most of the time rocking our inconsolable baby on the family swing. I sat on the periphery of our other boys' lives and watched them play without me. If I was feeling resentment toward this poor baby who cried incessantly and demanded so much of my energy, I have no doubt that our two other boys were begrudging him as well. This new baby took me away for long intervals, and when I did return, I was often too tired for energetic play. Respite care became essential to my sanity and helped give back our two older boys their mother—for at least part of the time. I had neighbours and friends take the baby as much as they were willing to. My parents joined me at the cottage for the summer. My husband often took over for me after sundown when he returned from work. We supplemented with formula so Daddy could give the baby a bottle in the evening, and I could devote some time to our other boys. It was imperative for them to realize that they too still belonged to Mom and were

Sibling Rivalry and Conflict Resolution

loved just as much. My husband and I did not want a situation where the older boys learned to envy their younger brother to the point of having no regard for him. Mothers with irritable babies are known to be at risk for depression, and forming a secure attachment with their infants in such cases can be obstructed. The circumstance demanded that we exhaust every resource we could to prevent either of those things from happening. A lot of the time that meant taking advantage of the support systems around us. In doing so, we managed to get through, and fortunately our relationships are intact.

> *"Rheanna, what do you want for your birthday?"*
> *"For you to stop talking to me!"*
>
> *Myles, age 5*
> *Rheanna, age 7*

Our boys have grown older, and although I would like to say we managed to thwart sibling rivalry, I have to admit that they spend a considerable amount of time in conflict, despite our best efforts during those early years. I have come to appreciate that tension between siblings is inevitable; however, I cling to the axiom that it will dissipate in time. When I think back, my two sisters and I fought constantly when we lived together. A chip in the plaster wall can still be seen in the room where my middle sister and I slept while growing up. One sister was running away from the other, who was chasing her with a raised fist and threatening to "knock her lights out." The middle sister flew onto the bed and slid athwart the sheets as if across home plate, slammed into the wall, chipping the plaster and gave herself a concussion.

Raking the lawn after my father had finished cutting the grass was always a chore divided up between me and my sisters. I usually got away with doing the least amount of work, being the youngest. One Saturday morning, my middle sister decided she had had enough of me not pulling my weight, and so she stuffed me inside the garbage bag amid the dew-sodden grass. I phoned my mother at work in complete hysterics and told her my sister had tried to kill me. We fought over just about everything: whose turn it was to do the dishes, dusting and vacuuming, borrowing clothes, and hogging the phone. Our boys do much the same. They fight over who has computer time, what to watch on TV, whose turn it is to set the table, and who has the best *Pokemon* cards. They fight for privacy and independence from one another. I have heard them say things like "I hate you" and "I wish you had never been born." But when they are separated, they find it hard to function—like amputees learning to adapt to the loss of a limb. I know how that feels too; when both my sisters moved out of the house when I was 14, I cried for weeks—I was so lonesome without them. My sisters are my best friends today, and we still have the odd disagreement. Conflict is inevitable. How we deal with that conflict is the key to resolution.

Teaching conflict resolution to children is a process that begins in infancy. What most parents do naturally for their children during the first few years of development has a great impact on the child's acquisition of conflict resolution skills later on. E. E. Maccoby (1980) identifies a number of different ways in which a parent can assist a child with the transition from impulsivity to self-control in her book entitled *Social Development: Psychological Growth and the Parent-Child Relationship*. Parents take much care in safeguarding their babies from becoming overwhelmed. They will limit the number of visitors and activity during the early days after birth. They dim lighting and control for loud noises. As their children become mobile, they protect them by imposing external limits on their surroundings so a curious child will not get into trouble. They put plastic safety measures over electrical outlets and gates in front of stairs. Parents soothe their child during emotional upsurges when the child lacks the internal skills to calm himself. They teach self-regulation through diversion of activities, like removing a screaming toddler from a stressful situation to an environment that offers an alternative activity. Parents give necessary information so the child can anticipate certain outcomes to his behaviour: "dirty, yucky, don't put that in your mouth"; "don't touch, *hot.*" Probably less intuitively in teaching self-restraint than the abovementioned, parents will also help train their child to delay gratification by not giving into his every whim, and they model self-control (which I will describe in more detail from my own experience in the next few paragraphs).Via these methods of support, parents can help move their children through a process of learning self-regulation. As the process evolves as the child gets older, the child will learn to control impulse tendencies and choose desirable, socially acceptable behaviours—not just because it is expected of him from his parents, but because he is morally, intrinsically motivated to choose right from wrong. Possessing self-restraint is particularly important in a social context with regard to interpersonal relations. What we tell our boys is that we don't always expect that they will get along, but when they do have disagreements, they need to find ways to problem-solve together—ways that are respectful and kind in relation to one another.

> *"Mommy, what did I do so wrong*
> *to cause you to have two more babies?"*
> *Alana, age 7*

We have rules of engagement in our house. My husband and I try to model these as best we can: allow the other person to explain their behaviour; respect the person's point of view (even if you don't agree with it); put yourself in the other person's shoes and imagine how he feels; use "I" messages to communicate expectations ("I don't like being shouted at because it hurts my feelings"); no name calling; you can't use the silent treatment (you can't resolve an issue if you're not talking about it); and work together to find a solution that will make it right. We are passionate in almost everything we do together, and arguing is no exception for how fervently we express ourselves to one another. So it's important for us to have rules; otherwise, we get carried away by the issue at hand and run the risk of leaving respect for one another behind. It's idealistic to think that we will follow all of these rules all of the time, but we try.

Couples who do not argue in front of their children, I think, are really doing them a disservice, unless the fighting is abusive toward one another, in which case it would be harmful for a child to witness, and the learning would contradict the teachings of conflict resolution. When parents argue fairly, they are modelling ways in which to cooperatively solve problems. Children imitate the actions of those people who influence them the most. If they do not see or hear their parents working together to resolve issues, they cannot effectively learn to deal with conflict in their own lives. They simply won't know how. Of course, there are issues and matters too private for little ears; I am talking about everyday stuff that comes up and causes friction between partners, such as leaving the gas tank empty, neglecting to put toilet paper on the roll, leaving dirty socks and underwear on the floor, not helping with household chores or who has domain over the remote control—issues as trivial and nonsensical as the things our children fight about.

Children observe their parents' interactions with each other, even when we don't think they're within earshot. My husband and I had an argument one time during those days of sleep deprivation. I look back on it now and realize I did not adhere to our rules of engagement, and neither did he. I became upset and frustrated, and knew I was losing control, so I left the house. I drove to the park and stopped the car. My husband called my cell phone, and when I answered, I could hear the two older boys crying in the background. The middle child was insisting his father tell me "sorry" so that I would come home. Of course, I had every intention of going home—but our son didn't know that. I began yelling at my husband, saying things I would regret, calling him names and swearing. Unfortunately, leaving the house did not prevent the boys from hearing my every word. I came through loud and clear over the telephone receiver—not a good example in modelling self-control.

If I could allow myself to become that irate, where I could feel the rage pumping through my body and could let it beat out a nasty rhythm in my tone and language, I cannot expect my boys to be more perfect than I when they become angry. It is my job as a parent to teach them self-control and respect for one another. I am responsible for their moral development. I want them to leave our house equipped with the necessary skills to have healthy, respectful relationships. I want them to have healthy relationships with each other. If I can't have that for myself and teach them to disrespect, ridicule and act in violence, then I have failed at the single most important job I will ever have. It is imperative, then, when I have mishandled a situation as badly as I did that argument, that I owe it to my children to admit that I have been wrong. Children learn by example. So when the example I have set is inappropriate, I have to take the learning from that mistake and teach it to my children. By *that* example, they will learn forgiveness.

We talked as a family how everybody felt that day—how each one of us was impacted by another's behaviour. My husband and I apologized to each other and took ownership for what part we played in the argument. We apologized to each of our boys for how we treated one another and in turn for how our unfair fighting made them feel. For what part the boys could contribute, we all worked together to find a solution. My husband and I took the more intimate details of the discussion off line and continued talking when we were alone, and calm. The boys witnessed a lot of affectionate gestures the next day between me and my husband. It was important for them to know that everything was all right again in their world and that their parents were safe.

I Am Sorry Story

I am sorry so I wrote this story,
To show my love for you.
You make me smile when I'm down,
My brother who never shows a frown.
If you weren't around,
I don't know what I'd do,
Because without you, I'd be blue.
I love you because you are you.
No matter what you do,
I love you.

Kohan, age 11

As parents, it is difficult to know when to get involved in sibling disputes. There are days when I can't stand the bickering, and the volume of shouting at each other is too much for me to bear. My husband's patience waxes and wanes as much as mine does; fortunately, when I am depleted of tolerance, my husband offers serenity, and vice versa. We try to approach every necessary intervention with respect for each child's point of view, remembering that the truth is in the eye of the beholder. A child is not necessarily lying about the accounts of any given situation; he is merely giving *his* interpretation of what happened. This often differs from the telling of events by the others involved. We have stopped asking for the truth. Instead, we give each child an opportunity to explain how he is feeling and what he needs from the other person. My husband and I don't get caught up in the content as much as we encourage our children to find a solution. Resolving conflicts independent of parental interference is the goal here. We try and reserve getting involved for those times when someone is going to be hurt—emotionally or physically. I abruptly interrupt name-calling, and there are consequences for causing physical harm to one another. When our boys inflict harm on one another, the doer has to make it up to the injured party by offering him a good deed. Our boys have written letters of apology, taken on each other's chores and given away personal valuables as a means of restitution.

As they go through this process of learning how to get along, they are developing negotiation and problem-solving skills. They fine-tune their consciences as they navigate between what is right and wrong. They attain healthy self-esteem when interactions are positive, and they feel good about the choices they make. They are learning about empathy and what it means to be respectful. As they begin to subscribe to a higher order of moral reasoning, they will factor in all sides of an argument, not just their own. All encompassing, they ascertain self-control.

"Kohan call me stupid! That's not nice, no!"
Talen, age 3

It had been a day of conflict. It started out pleasant enough. The two older boys were playing a game of checkers at the kitchen table. They rarely engage in organized play so, when it does happen, I like to observe how well they *can* get along. The pleasantries only lasted as long as it took for one of them to cheat and the other to start calling names. Within a few minutes, the game turned ugly, and checkers were being hurled at one another. I asked them to work it out. They ignored me. I reminded them of how we speak to one another in this family and suggested they take a break from the game and return to it when they were both calm. The insults back and forth only continued. I employed one of Barbara Coloroso's (2001) brilliant parenting strategies from her book *Kid's are Worth it!*, where I had them sit side-by-side until they gave each other permission to get up from the table. The idea is to get them to cool down and start talking to one another. They can't effectively problem-solve together if they are too angry to talk to each other. By giving one another permission to get up, they are also forgiving one another. The eldest always holds out much longer than our middle child. It was 20 minutes before they both could leave the table, and, for a time after, they went their separate ways.

The venue changed for the afternoon, and so did the soldiers of battle. This time, the youngest brother was being ostracized by his older siblings. They refused to let him join them in their tree fort. I can't imagine what the neighbours must have thought when they heard this pint-sized munchkin screaming at the top of his lungs and hitting the trunk of the tree with a giant stick. I had to go outside because it was getting violent. The little one had gotten his hands on a bungee cord from the shed and was whipping it at his brothers. The oldest had been genuinely afraid of being hit and had run back into the cottage. The middle child tried to defend himself by throwing crab apples at his small, but mighty opponent, hitting him in the chest. The youngest acts like a tough guy most of the time, but when he's hurt, he falls in a puddle at my feet, beseeching comfort. I picked him up, noting the red mark in the middle of his torso, and began shouting for a truce. It was then that I crossed into enemy territory. I was accused of taking the younger one's side—again! The middle child stomped away, muttering something about always being blamed for things. The eldest conveniently made himself scarce, forsaking any responsibility, and the little one continued to wail at the unfairness of the situation.

Resigned, I abandoned my peaceful afternoon of writing, to play bus station with my youngest child on the family swing. Thinking my two older children would recognize their newfound freedom and re-conquer their tree fort, I was astounded when they appeared, waiting by the swing's platform. The youngest brother enthusiastically stopped the "bus" and asked his brothers if they needed a ride somewhere. The two of them eagerly accepted his invitation and the four of us played many rounds of dropping off and picking up passengers along an imaginary route, and we all managed to get along.

> *"Sorry, guys, I can't come over. I promised my brother I would play with him this afternoon."*
> *Kohan, age 11*

So sibling rivalry never really ends. But it will get better as they practice and fine-tune the problem-solving skills taught to them. As they become more efficient at conflict resolution, it will take less and less time for them to resolve their differences. In the interim, while we are waiting for them to stop the constant fighting, we can think about every conflict as an opportunity for growth. Every squabble is a chance for them to test out new ways to negotiate and reason with one another. Think about it as an investment in their future. As tiring as it seems right now, siblings are learning valuable lessons that will only serve them favourably in the years yet to come. Think of how many personality conflicts you, or a friend or a relative have had with co-workers, neighbours or friends. Think about those situations that were successful in resolution. Those were the times when we did most of our learning—whether it was in relation to one another, personally or professionally. We want those same experiences for our children. As parents, we owe it to them to teach them to effectively problem-solve. There is no better training ground than in the arena of sibling rivalry.

We may not always like some of the people we work with; we may find our neighbours irritating, and we may even have a hard time relating with our partners. We don't always have to get along, but we do have to find ways to problem-solve together—ways that are respectful and kind in relation to one another. When we put that into practice ourselves, we instinctively teach it to our children.

6
Sexuality

"Mommy, I want to marry you."
Talen, age 4

It is when our children are babies that we have the first opportunities to teach them about love and trust in relationships. Through attachment parenting, parents communicate love by responding to their babies' cues to be held, comforted, fed and changed. They speak softly to their infant and frequently offer affection through healthy touch. They rub their baby's back, smooth out his hair, caress his little hands and feet and kiss his podgy cheeks often. It is in these early moments of nurturing when children discover what it feels like to be loved. Such demonstrations of affection teach children how to love in turn. They first reveal their feelings for Mommy and Daddy and then extend their show of affection toward other family members and relatives and, eventually to people outside their nuclear family. I can remember the first time each one of my boys spontaneously reached out for me to give me a hug and a kiss. A shift in each of our relationships happened then. The child was no longer just a receiver of my attentiveness but was learning how to love back.

Infants gain a sense of security in the love that they feel. They begin to develop a concept of self and of others by internalizing the interactions they have with their caretakers. They interpret their parents' devotion to them and begin to trust that their parents will take care of their needs. This developed trust is the foundation for being able to aptly relate with others later on in

71

life. If a trusting relationship is not cultivated, then bonding is less likely to occur. If a child has not healthily attached as an infant, then his ability to experience intimacy in romantic relationships as an adult is hindered.

In 1978, Mary Ainsworth and a group of research associates identified three patterns of infant-caregiver attachment behaviour, which they categorized as *secure, anxious* and *avoidant*. Almost 10 years later, three investigators, Shaver, Hazan and Bradshaw first conceptualized these behaviours of attachment as being predictors of intimacy in adult romantic relationships: *Attachment security* lends itself to intimacy, sharing, considerate communication and openness to sexual exploration. *Attachment anxiety* results in fears of rejection and abandonment, making it difficult to commit to another person and *attachment avoidance* interferes with a person's ability to get intimate and physically close with someone.

Little did we know that when we were bonding with our babies, that we were setting them up to have successful romantic relationships as adults.

> *"When my grow up, my gonna have a BIG penis."*
> *"Yes, you will!"*
>
> Nolan, age 3
> Emily, age 3½

Infancy is also the earliest time when parents are given the chance to model a positive attitude toward sexuality. Babies naturally explore and play with their bodies. Anyone who has ever changed a diaper knows this to be true. How we react to these early signs of sexual curiosity in our children will set the tone for how our children develop their own thoughts and feelings about sex. I once received a call from our young in-house nanny in the middle of a workday. She was a little embarrassed and had a hard time initially telling me why she had called. She had been changing my son's diaper and was shocked to see that he had an erection. The intent of her call was to know if this was normal for a child of seven months and to ask what she should do when he kept grabbing himself. Like I had, our nanny had grown up with sisters. She had had limited exposure to little boys and was not well educated on their anatomy. Once I reassured her that it was perfectly natural for baby boys to have erections and to want to touch themselves, she then felt better equipped to handle the situation. Our nanny learned to deal with these episodes with a matter-of-fact attitude. She carried on with the task at hand, of changing his diaper, but did not bring attention to him wanting to touch himself. Simply, she gently moved his hand out of the way so that she could finish changing him. She did not tell him to stop or give him the impression that he was wrong or bad for what he was doing, which may have resulted in shaming my son. If a child learns through the reactions of his parents or caregiver that sex is taboo, then he will inherit feelings of guilt and shame and think he is abnormal for responding to the natural cues his body gives him.

When our boys reached an age (around three) where they began to understand that if they rubbed their penis it got bigger, then they were told that their bodies were special and did wonderful things in response to loving touch. This is the time to teach children about healthy touch from others. Our boys were told Mommy and Daddy and the names of other caregivers who could help them wash in the bathtub. They were instructed that bathing was the only time that anybody should be touching their penises, with the exception of their doctor under certain circumstances. Each of them was told that it was okay for him to touch his own penis—after all, it belonged to him—but that there was a time and a place for that. We began introducing the concept of privacy. We taught them to knock on closed doors and had them shut the door when they were in the bathroom. Instead of putting their hands down their pants in public whenever the urge struck them, they learned to retreat to their rooms. They began to understand what inappropriate sexual behaviour in front of others was, but at the same time learned that it was acceptable for them to explore their own bodies in private. This distinction became more apparent around the age of four, when they began telling me not to look at them if I was helping them to change into pyjamas. They didn't care if Dad saw them—he has the same parts. They insisted on washing themselves in the bathtub and preferred their father take them to a public washroom instead of having to go into the ladies' room. They no longer announced to the world that their "penis was hard" or embarrassed their father in the change room at the local pool by commenting on the size of his genitals. They learned to set limits on their behaviour by inhibiting the natural psychosexual responses of their bodies and controlling them within the norms of private exploration.

> *"She really likes her Barbie dolls.*
> *I don't know how to play that."*
> *Kohan, age 3*

As babies grow into toddlers, they begin to identify the differences between boys and girls—not just with respect to anatomy but also how male and female roles and expectations differ. Society plays a huge part in projecting gender differences onto young people, right from infancy. We dress baby boys in blue and girls in pink. We roughhouse with our preschool boys and sit and colour with our girls. We give meaning to these differences by practicing them over and over again. Through the evolution of time, the progression toward what men and women can do has become more favourable for women. It is becoming more commonplace for women to take on roles that were traditionally male. We don't flinch so much anymore when we see women playing male-dominated sports or anchoring on a sports television network and going into the men's dressing room to conduct interviews. We watch a former first-lady run for the candidacy of president of the United States and say "why not?" Yet we still have difficulty embracing the concept of stay-at-home dads, male nurses and men who design clothes or style hair.

The other day, while setting out clothes for our youngest to go to day care, he noticed that on the inside of the shirt I chose for him there was pink binding securing the edges of the garment. It had presumably been red but had faded in the wash. He absolutely refused to wear it, telling me that "boys don't wear pink, and everyone is going to laugh at me." I tried to convince him that it was on the inside of the shirt and that no one was even going to see it. But he knew it was there and was evidently quite disturbed by it. I was in a hurry to get out the door and had little patience for this so I just tossed him another shirt and asked him to get dressed. It was our eldest son who had the wisdom to say that "real men can wear pink" but it unfortunately had little impact on his youngest sibling, who began crying that his brother was making fun of him.

On my drive to work, I couldn't help but wonder where his opinion about the colour pink had come from. Gender colour assignment has never been an issue in our house—I am the only girl! In fact, when our eldest son was two years old, his favourite pyjamas were a pink pair of Winnie-the-Pooh that he got as a hand-me-down from his older female cousin. Our son adored this cousin—still does. He was so proud to wear anything that had once belonged to her. They were made from the softest flannel and felt so comfortable against his skin; it's no wonder he loved to wear them. Our middle child wore black-and-white pyjamas with 101 Dalmatians with pink bows around their necks. He's crazy about dogs. Those pj's were of exceedingly good quality, and I passed them onto my sister-in-law for her son to wear. She returned them to me shortly afterward, saying her husband refused to let their son put them on.

We live in a country where our women's Olympic hockey team has won two consecutive gold medals. Some of our most accomplished musicians and composers are women. We have had a female prime minister. And yet, we are still teaching our boys that they cannot wear pink!

> *"Michael has a vagina in the shape of a ponytail."*
> *Lilly, age 4*

It is important that we give our children the proper names for their body parts and the parts of the opposite sex as well. It makes it less confusing when they need to tell you something of a sexual nature. It also helps when formal talk about sexuality becomes necessary—then the awkwardness over introducing such terms and labelling sexual organs will have been thwarted through the ease of use over time. You wouldn't go into a gynaecological appointment telling the physician that there was something wrong with your *wee wee*, would you? From the ages of two to five, children are naturally curious about their bodies and the bodies of the opposite sex. They simply respond to the cues their bodies give them and naturally explore through touch to find out more. Boys get penile erections and girls produce vaginal secretions as early as the third trimester of pregnancy, while they are still in their mother's womb. A child's innocence is not inhibited by societal norms of what is sexually permissible and appropriate. A preschooler will ask a peer to "show me yours, and I'll show you mine" and not think it is wrong to do so. Children play doctor, and they discover the differences between male and female anatomies. It's imperative that parents don't overreact in these situations.

These opportunities give us the chance to reiterate our teachings about privacy and respect for others and about healthy touch. When we go over the top, lecturing about sin and immorality, we inject shame and guilt into our children. What they learn then, is that sexual behaviour is immoral and that they are bad people for responding to the cues of their bodies. When I was working in child and adolescent psychiatry, I did a short stint working on the phones in the intake department. This is where calls are received from people with potential referrals for psychiatric services. I received a call once from a mother requesting rape counselling for her three-year-old daughter. She said that her daughter had been sexually molested by her four-year-old nephew. The children had been playing in the backyard alone, and when the mother went to check on them, she found them both naked, and the boy was touching the girl's genitals. I know how hysterical she was with me on the phone; I can just imagine how she reacted to those children when she saw what they were doing in the backyard. It would have been the simplest thing to put this case down to a couple of kids "playing doctor" and to tell the mother to relax. However, the mother's reaction to this situation needed to be explored. It was important to discern whether or not the young boy had been exposed to explicit sexual content, which would explain his actions as being beyond that of a typical four-year-old. In that case, the boy was at risk, and other agencies needed to get involved. If he was acting normal, given his age and stage of development, then the mother needed to understand that. And if that were the case, this mother was at risk of damaging her daughter's development of a healthy view of sexuality because of how she responded. Either way, this mother needed education, so counselling for her was warranted.

Before calling in the cavalry and interviewing the children, we brought the mother in and talked with her. What she described in witnessing was a typical scene of two children innocently curious about each other's bodies. Neither of them had any reason to believe that what they were doing was unacceptable because they hadn't had any formal teachings about sexuality, privacy and respect. There was no previous concern for her nephew's well-being. There were no other behavioural signs that he was being sexually abused or had been exposed to pornography. Although the mother remained incredibly uncomfortable with what she had seen, she did come to the realization that her nephew did not "molest" her daughter—at least not in a perverted way. He was acting out his natural curiosity to find out more about a member of the opposite sex, and her little girl, equally curious, went along with it. This mother was given resources on psychosexual development of young children and was coached on how to go back and revisit the issue with her daughter from a developmental teaching standpoint.

> *"That baby has a penis.*
> *My mommy has a bagina with a hole in it."*
> *Nolan, age 3*

Just as important as naming body parts correctly for our children, is taking care to answer their questions honestly. We start having conversations about sex with our children from the very first question they ask, which usually comes between the ages of two and three. I can still see the expression on our boys' grandparents' faces when each of them was asked whether they had a penis or a vagina. Our middle child was particularly curious about this question and would even ask unsuspecting patrons in the grocery checkout. We need to be honest, but to a point that matches the child's developmental stage. Just because our son was curious to distinguish the differences between males and females, and the distinguishing factor for him was the penis, it did not mean that he wanted to know what the penis was used for. It helps to clarify what the child is asking and to give him only the information that he is seeking. As they grow and their questions become more complex, we can provide them with information that they are more able to process, given their developmental age. When they are really young, keep it short and simple. When our middle son was three, he asked me how babies got out of their mommies' tummies. He already knew that females had vaginas, so I explained that there was an opening in the vagina, and the baby came out from there. At three years old, I did not think it was necessary to give him any of the technical terms like uterus and cervix. He didn't ask me how babies got in there so I didn't tell him that either. When we handle their questioning with respect and give them honest answers, we create an atmosphere that promotes lifelong communication about sexuality. So when the difficult questions come, they won't hesitate to ask us.

Recently I was at a work conference where a group of women got together for some drinks in the evening. The conversation led to sex, as it inevitably does, and one of the ladies used a sexual phrase that I had never heard of. I put it out to the group that what this person had said was unfamiliar to me and that I wanted to know what it meant. There was a lot of laughter and some high school kind of bantering that went on before one brave soul explained to me, in rather graphic detail, what the phrase implied. It took a minute or two to process the complexity of it and, as I did this, I noticed there were a few others who looked just as perplexed as I was. I have a sneaky suspicion that I wasn't the only one in that group who didn't know the said term. But I was the only who admitted to not knowing what it was and the only one who asked for clarification. So, if I was the only one who didn't understand, why was there only one person who volunteered to enlighten me?

When we are teaching our children about sexuality, we need to make sure that we are comfortable with the questions they ask and are prepared to answer them in a sincere way. If we shame them for asking and waffle on the details, then we leave them to their own devices. When they are little, they will use their imaginations and make up what they do not understand. As they get older, they will seek their information elsewhere and run the risk of not being properly informed. Misinformation leads to sexual promiscuity, teenage pregnancy and the contraction of sexually transmitted diseases. We need to protect our children from these fates by giving them accurate knowledge.

"I think your voice just cracked."
"Yeah, I must be starting puberty."
Father, age 40-something
Nolan, age 9

The question remains of when the appropriate time is that we start teaching our children about the fundamentals of sexuality.

I don't know if there is a magic age when our children should be taught. Our school board sends home a pamphlet on sexuality and reproduction at the end of grade five, suggesting that age nine or ten would be an appropriate time. My husband and I hadn't any formal discussion with our eldest son about sexuality prior to his bringing home the information from school. We had handled any questions he had with honesty and sincerity along the way but realized in retrospect that the questions had stopped being asked around the age of seven or eight. I approached him one day at the beginning of grade six and asked if he would like to read the pamphlet together and was shocked by his response. He became red in the face and took an angry tone with me, saying that he was not interested. I defaulted to my husband, thinking that perhaps it was a mother-son thing. He responded to his father with the same embarrassment and ambivalence.

While visiting my sister-in-law, I learned that my nine-year-old niece has already been well informed by her parents about the "birds and the bees." My sister has always been open about menstruation and reproduction with her two children from the time they were old enough to talk. I have to admit, I sometimes thought perhaps my niece and nephew had a little too much information too soon. Conceivably, I was wrong—her children are certainly not embarrassed to talk to her about sex. A daughter of a friend of mine started menstruating at age nine. The onset of menses appears to be happening so much earlier for young girls these days than when I was growing up and the average age was 13. Her daughter was prepared, having been told about puberty prior to that first rite of passage to becoming a woman. If my son were female, he would not have been ready, and his father and I would have been at fault for that.

Perhaps my husband and I waited too long to have those discussions with our eldest son. Now that our son realizes everyone else in his class already knows all this stuff, he may have gotten the impression that we were too uncomfortable to talk with him about sex. He may have inadvertently gotten the message that sex is something to be ashamed of, thus feeling embarrassed now when we bring it up. But then again, his reluctance to have this conversation with us now might just be because of his temperament. Our eldest son has always been private with his thoughts, whereas our middle child wears them on his sleeve. At nine years old, our second-born continues to ask questions—sensitive questions that provoke a lot of discussion. I think the important thing is to assess the individual character of your child and discern how much information he can handle at a particular stage of development. What I've learned through this situation is that just because our eldest child stopped asking the questions didn't mean he was not curious. Be open and honest, and check in periodically to see where your child is at in terms of needing information. Don't wait to talk about sex until a time when you think he is old enough to understand. By then, he may be too embarrassed to talk about it with you.

7

Discipline

"Talen, if you continue doing that, I will have to take you out."
"So you want to kill me?"

Father, age 40-something
Talen, age 4½

As a parent educator, I have facilitated many workshops on discipline. I always kick off the seminar by asking the parent attendees what it is that they want for their children. In the numerous discussion groups I have led, the list I extract is basically the same. Parents want their children to be independent, motivated, self-assured, moral, successful, healthy, safe, respectful and content. They want their children to know right from wrong, to think for themselves and make good decisions, to be accountable for their behaviours, to have healthy relationships and to be proud of who they are.

After the list is compiled, I then ask the participants how they go about ensuring that their children develop these characteristics. The answer I hear most emphatically is "discipline." The confusing part for most of us is to discern what discipline entails. I have found it helpful to make a distinction between the words *punishment* and *discipline*. According to the *Webster's Ninth New Collegiate Dictionary*, the word punishment means *suffering, pain or loss that serves as retribution. A penalty inflicted on an offender; severe, rough or disastrous treatment.* In contrast, the word discipline means *teaching, learning. Training that corrects, moulds or perfects the mental faculties or moral character.* The key difference lies in the implication of the word *teaching*. Discipline provides an opportunity for learning. When a parent disciplines a child, he teaches that child *why* his behaviour is unacceptable and offers alternative ways in which the child should behave. With punishment, children only come to expect that, for certain behaviours, there are negative consequences that cause physical and or emotional pain. Considering the list we formulated on what we want for our children, I have never had parents say that they wanted their children to be harmed or to suffer emotional pain. When a child is punished, he is given no understanding for why his behaviour is wrong, nor is he taught how to correct it. We wonder why then our children repeatedly make the same mistakes, without having learned from their punishment.

So now that we have a clear understanding of what the goal of discipline is—an opportunity for us to teach our children—we need to come up with some concrete strategies that fit within that premise. I then ask parents what corrective measures do they make use of, and I list them on a flip chart under the categories "discipline" and "punishment." I write many of the responses on the line dividing the two words and explain that, depending on how the corrective methods are executed, they are either on one side or the other. I am usually offered a wide spectrum of suggestions for how parents attempt to correct their children's behaviour. They range from giving choices, logical and natural consequences, talking, listening, parental modelling and praise to time outs, taking away privileges, reward systems, grounding, bribing, ignoring, yelling, threatening and spanking. This is not a comprehensive list, but it is what I hear most consistently from parents. At a bird's-eye view, it appears relatively simple to distinguish which ones belong under which category, but as we go through them, we quickly learn that it's not as easy as it looks. This is probably why we struggle so much with effectively disciplining our children.

> *"Talen, you're angry. I use to be just like that when I was a kid. You have to learn that building with Lego takes time and patience."*
>
> *Nolan, age 9*

I will first go through the strategies that I think sit on the fence between discipline and punishment. How a parent goes about implementing each of these corrective measures will determine whether it disciplines a child or punishes him. *Grounding* and *taking away privileges* are not necessarily punishments by nature—unless they do not give life to learning for the child. For instance, our middle child had once misbehaved while Christmas shopping at the mall. I had gone off in one direction, and my husband had taken our two older children to the food court to get something to eat. The boys were around five and three years of age at the time. While eating, the three-year-old would not stay seated in his chair but took much pleasure in crawling under the table and eating French fries that had been left on the floor by earlier patrons. My husband repeatedly told him to stop. His father explained that the French fries were dirty and may make him sick and if he did not listen he would have to go home and would therefore not have a chance to see Santa Claus. After hearing his father say it three or four times but not act on it, our son learned very quickly that his father was not going to follow through; it was an idle threat. So, the misbehaviour continued after leaving the food court in the form of our son initiating a game of hide-and-seek. He would run away, causing his father to chase after him, our other son in tow.

Once they met up with me, we decided it would be easier to divide the children between us. My husband, having had enough, gave me the responsibility for our second-born. While trying to make it through a crowd of people to get to another store, our son resumed his game of hide-and-seek and took off in hot pursuit of the best secret place to conceal himself. I lost him among a row of kiosks and frantic holiday shoppers. I began to call out his name and, when he didn't answer me, I went straight to panic. A dozen or more people gathered around to hear a description of what he was wearing and looked like and, before too long, he was returned to me. He had ducked into a women's clothing store and hidden inside a rack of dresses. As relieved as I was to see him, I was also furious. I took him by the hand and began walking him out of the mall and told him we unfortunately now could not see Santa because we were going to find Daddy and go home. In protest, he began shouting at the top of his lungs, "Help me; don't let this person take me away!" By this time, my husband had reappeared. He picked up our screaming son, hoisted him over his shoulder and took him out to the parking lot. There, he sat in our vehicle with his father and waited while I took his brother to see Santa.

The privilege of seeing Santa Claus was not taken from our son at random. He acted up in the mall before we got to Santa's village. We could not continue shopping when he was putting himself at risk of getting lost, and therefore he had to wait in the car until his brother was finished seeing Santa Claus. It would have been unfair to take away the privilege from our other son; he had behaved in the mall. Having to leave the mall resulted in our three-year-old not seeing Santa; it was in direct correlation to his behaviour. In this instance, the loss of privilege made sense, and the learning for our son was that when you are behaving in ways that are unsafe, you cannot expect to be allowed to stay and continue—even if you haven't yet received the treat your mom and dad promised. The alternative behaviour taught is that you need to stay close to mom and dad when you are out in public. That's discipline.

If we had taken the opportunity for him to see Santa away as a result of his hitting his brother, the connection between cause and effect would have been harder for him to make. The message would have been that he was not worthy of seeing Santa because he hit his brother. Not feeling worthy is emotionally painful. That's punishment. In this example, there had been no alternative taught to replace his unacceptable conduct.

Without learning substitute behaviours for expressing anger and frustration, it is plausible that he would hit his brother again in the absence of knowing what else to do, particularly when it was no longer Christmas and the threat of not seeing Santa was remote. Similarly, if we would have chosen to ground him from his next two play dates instead of taking him home from the mall before he saw Santa, he would probably run amuck the next time he was out in public, not having learned that it is unsafe to do so. Grounding *can* be a suitable form of discipline when it is age-appropriate and directly connects with the misbehaviour. I tell parents when a child can conceptualize time, then grounding can work in certain situations. Consequences should be delivered as close as possible to the misbehaviour, especially for a young child. When a child cannot conceive how much time has lapsed between the incident and the disciplinary action imposed, then the lesson is lost on him. He won't get it when you remind him three days later that he cannot go to his friend's house to play because he acted up at the mall on the weekend. Conversely, a nine-year-old who crossed a busy intersection on his bike will make the connection between his unsafe behaviour and having to stay close to home for the next couple of days.

I would be remiss if I did not mention how we addressed the scene where our son was yelling for help in the mall, indicating that I was a stranger taking him away. Once we returned home and everyone was calm, we talked about his unsafe behaviour. His running away and hiding could result in his being lost or abducted. We told him that if I was a stranger, then yelling to alert people *would* be the appropriate thing to do, but it is extremely important to only say that if I was a stranger. We reminded him of the story *Peter and the Wolf.* We listened to his rationale for why he did what he did, all the while respecting his point of view and understanding his perception. He thought by saying that I was a stranger, someone would take him from me and then he would be able to stay at the mall and see Santa. Well, that made sense—for a three-year-old. We clarified that he did not see Santa Claus then, because he was acting unsafe, and, as a result, we had to leave the mall. The loss of that privilege was because of his behaviour in the mall, and it did not apply to any other chance our son had to see Santa. The following weekend, the neighbours were going on a sleigh ride. Refreshments were being offered afterward, and Santa was going to make an appearance. We accepted the invitation to go along, and our son got to see The Big Guy there. I can't remember how long it was before he accompanied us shopping again. I do remember that the moment he started to stray from us, he only needed to be reminded of having to leave the mall, and then there were no further problems.

> *"I don't want to go on time-out. Maybe you*
> *should go back to babysitting school."*
> *Kohan, age 6*

Time-out has revolutionized parenting. Since it's inception in the literature in the late 1950s, it has been accepted as a non-punitive form of scolding and is the most widely researched discipline procedure. It has become the most commonly used tactic parents resort to when attempting to change a child's behaviour. It is also the one strategy that is most often used incorrectly and, for that reason, it sits on the fence between discipline and punishment. The numerous published articles regarding time-out refer to it as the removal of available rewards from a child who is misbehaving. The focus is on promoting self-calming skills. Unfortunately, we have taken this relatively simple concept and injected it with so many rules for its use that we have rendered it ineffective and punitive. One misconception is that parents think that they should warn the child a few times of a pending time-out. In doing so, the child only learns that he has at least a few more chances before Mom or Dad follows through. Parents then wonder why it takes yelling at their kids three or four times to get them to listen. Another mistake is that parents feel compelled to lecture their child on the way to time-out, and they continue to remind the child while he is in time-out why he is there. The child is either too upset to take in any information or learns to tune the parent out, therefore missing the point of the lecture. Parents also have the erroneous belief that the child must say "I'm sorry" after the time-out has been served. My nephew was so accustomed to apologizing every time he did something wrong, that when my sister asked him "what do you say?" after his grandmother gave him a birthday present, he answered, "I'm sorry." The other risk with making kids apologize for everything is that they begin to think it is a one-way ticket out of trouble. How often have you heard an apology that sounded insincere? The words are used so often in so many different situations that they have lost their meaning. Parents also think that they have to apply time restrictions to the time-out's duration; one minute for every year of age seems to be the standard, when in fact, the research literature suggests that shorter time-outs are generally more effective than longer ones. If we want our children to be independent and think for themselves, we have to give them opportunities to learn how to do that. They need to be the ones to decide when they are ready to come off time-out. I certainly would not appreciate if I were upset, and my husband told me I had 40 minutes to calm down and then insist I come back and say I'm sorry. Forty minutes may be too long for me in one instance and not enough time in another circumstance. The other horrible thing we parents do is think that we physically have to remove the child from our presence, when, in fact, "sit and watch time-out's" are more effective. Keeping the child in close proximity to the parent does not threaten the child's sense of attachment. I have often found it necessary to sit alongside my child who has been removed from a situation to help him through his tears. Just knowing that I am there makes it easier for him to cry, and adapt, so he can return to whatever it was that he was doing in the first place. Another mistake parents yield is making the time-out more about the chair or the stair or the naughty corner, and we forget about the self-quieting aspect. I know parents who have dragged their child to the time-out seat and sat on him to make him stay there. I still know people who think it's acceptable to have their child face the corner. When we are shaming and ridiculing our children, we cannot expect them to adapt to the situation and come out smiling and deliver a heartfelt apology—their hearts have been broken.

> *"Emily, how was your day?"*
> *"I played at my friend's house. Mommy came to get me, and I didn't want to go so I stomped on her foot. She said, 'blah, blah, blah,' and then I had a time-out."*
> Father, age 30-something
> Emily, age 4

From a meta-analysis of several hundred published studies conducted by Edward Christophersen and Susan Mortweet VanScoyoc (2007), six general guidelines for setting up a successful time-out were identified. *1. Provide an enriched nurturing environment.* Time-out will only work if the child has something to compare it to. The phrase "catch your child being good" has become quite popular in the last while. The premise is to focus on a child's good behaviour and to not always dwell on the negative. Time-out works more effectively if a child is used to getting positive attention consistently throughout the day. It may come in the form of verbal praise, a pat on the back, a wink or thumbs up, a hug or a smile. The time-out or withdrawal of available rewards will then seem so drastic in comparison to how he is usually treated. If a child is always being yelled at, ignored and belittled, then time-out will not have that much effect on him. It just becomes more of the same in the life of that child. *2. Keep instruction for time-out short and unemotional.* No warnings. No mini-lectures. If you have communicated something to your child once, then you should not have to repeat yourself. If you find that you have to ask him again, that is when the time-out should be delivered. *3. Do not provide any attention during time-out.* Do not talk to your child when he is in time-out. Let him cry, scream, stomp his feet or whatever (as long as he is safe from harming himself). Ignore the antics—do not feed into his negative behaviour, even if you do choose to sit down beside him. The idea is to help him to self-regulate. Ignoring outside of time-out can also be effective with behaviours such as whining or back-talking. When the child sees he is not getting a reaction out

e

of you and is told how he can appropriately get your attention, he will disengage his efforts and choose a more desirable way to interact with you. Ignoring becomes punishment when a child comes into your presence and, for whatever reason, you neglect to acknowledge him or refuse to listen when he needs to talk with you. *4. Focus on building self-quieting skills versus a time limit.* Children should only stay in time-out for as long as it takes for them to regroup. I empower my children to decide when they have mustered enough composure to return to whatever it was that got them into trouble. When you allow your child the freedom to determine his readiness, you will undoubtedly get the child who will claim that he is able to return when you can still see the smoke coming out of his ears. I gently ask him to think about it again and point out that he still looks angry. Sometimes, in teaching children how to read their own bodies, you have to let them go and find out that they indeed were not ready, which often means a repeat time-out. This way, they learn to interpret the signals of their own bodies (heart rate slows, breathing and pulse return to normal), and begin to recognize when they do feel better. *5. Use other strategies to teach new skills.* Time-out should not be used for a child who manifests misbehaviour because he has not yet mastered a new skill, such as toilet training, sharing, tying shoes or getting dressed. *6. Always be consistent.*

Although the research findings do not address what happens after time-out, I think it's an important aspect in the sequence of learning. I am a huge advocate for replacing undesirable behaviours with acceptable ones. I do not think that a child will learn to do anything different in similar situations if he has not been given suggestions for what he could do instead. When my children have come off time-out, we take the opportunity to discuss the event and together decide what they could do differently the next time.

> *"I'll do it if you pay me. Other kids in my class get*
> *paid for doing this kind of stuff."*
>
> *Nolan, age 8*

I spent a great deal of time expressing my opinion about *reward systems* in chapter 2 with regards to toilet training. It is clear that I see the use of rewards to teach new skills as a detriment to a child's self-esteem and therefore consider it a measure of punishment. However, on the flip side of using rewards to control a child's behaviour, they can be an effective disciplinary tool, in terms of providing positive reinforcement. The caveat is *when* a parent offers and delivers a reward. If the reward is contingent upon the behaviour—if you get an A on that test, your father and I will buy you a baseball glove—the child learns to be extrinsically motivated. He is then not interested in doing well because it feels good inside or because it will boost his opinion of himself or make him feel proud of who he is and proud of his accomplishments. Instead, he performs solely for the acquisition of a coveted prize. If the prize isn't big or interesting enough, he is less inclined to perform. Using rewards to help provide an enriched, nurturing environment, looks very different from using rewards to get an expected response from your child. A reward is praise for a job well done, or for good behaviour or just because you love your kid.

Once, sometimes twice, a year, I take one boy at a time out of school and do something special with him—not for any reason in particular, just because I want to celebrate the exceptional boy he is. I have taken them swimming, out for lunch, to a movie and skiing. I don't announce I'm going to do this until the day of the surprise. There are no limitations for getting to go, and nor are there requirements that need to be fulfilled afterward. I reward them simply for being who they are. Not all rewards have to have a monetary value either. My husband will often take one of the boys to his work on a Saturday morning. They spend time looking over the job site, talking and enjoying each other's company. The boys look so forward to spending this time with their father, and, more often than not, they haven't spent a dime during those outings. My husband and I have rewarded accomplishments too—as an afterthought. We do not bribe our children into behaving the way we want them to; when they behave correctly, it is because it is the right thing to do, and they feel good about that.

Our middle child has been diagnosed with a reading disorder. He seeks extra help through the local learning disabilities association, where he goes twice a week. It's a lot of work. Last year, when his course came to an end, we took him out for pizza—not because he was promised that if he did really well, he would receive a reward. We simply wanted to recognize his hard work and give him a pat on the back for trying his best. We wanted to let him know that we appreciate how much he struggles to learn to read, and taking him out for pizza was the gesture that helped us communicate our pride in his efforts. It also helped him to celebrate his own success. He had no idea we were planning a dinner in his honour, and he worked hard anyway.

> *"Momma, what's wrong with your ears? I can see*
> *you standing there; why can't you hear me?"*
> *Ava, age 2½*

Many parents are enlightened to hear that the way in which they have been implementing a disciplinary technique has actually been counterproductive in displacing misbehaviour and, as a result, their child has been punished instead. They leave the workshop with a renewed sense that, if executed correctly, the method will work to teach the child acceptable alternatives to his misbehaviour. Some parents are less encouraged. They explain it necessary to resort to a more authoritarian style of parenting and need to be convinced that those strategies listed under punishment are harmful to a child and do very little to correct behaviour. Spanking (including a slap on the hand) is one of those methods that spark a lot of controversy.

There are opposing views in the literature as to whether or not spanking is abusive and will lead to violent behaviour in children. The research against spanking has been criticised for not making a clear distinction between a slap on the butt and obvious abuse. It has been argued that, when clear cases of abuse are not excluded from research studies on spanking, the results are skewed and therefore no evidence can be found that spanking by a loving parent causes harm to a child. I can't debate the flaws in any of the research findings—I am not a research analyst. I can't win that argument. So I have to pose the question in such a way that gets parents thinking about spanking as a disciplinary measure used to teach children. I ask parents to consider the list that we developed at the beginning of the workshop—what do they want for their children? If they think the only way for their children to attain those characteristics is by spanking them, then I challenge that belief with the following story: A colleague and I were attending a conference at a large hotel that was also playing host to a number of tourist groups. We were waiting in a crowded vestibule for an elevator that seemed to be taking forever. One of the tour guides was standing in between the two elevators holding a clipboard, blocking the elevators' indicator light on the control panel. My colleague was curious as to whether the button had been pushed or not and gently excused herself and reached in behind the tour guide's clipboard. What happened next was unfathomable; the tour guide turned around and slapped my colleague's hand. The crack reverberated throughout the narrow foyer, and several gasps could be heard by a number of witnesses. I couldn't help but ask the rhetorical question: "Did he just slap you?" I will never forget the look on my co-worker's face. She was flushed with red and white blotches, her eyes were glistening with tears of disbelief and her mouth was lax. Her silence was in stark contrast to my outrage. I started yelling at the man, and he in turn shouted back at me. The elevator came, and my colleague, still in shock, gestured that we wait for the next one. The crowd of people poured through the open doors and descended, leaving the two of us standing there absolutely bewildered. She was humiliated and angry—not to mention confused as to what she should do next.

When I tell this story, I ask how many people in the audience think my associate was assaulted. The vast majority will raise their hands. Some people have not viewed the slap as harsh enough to be considered assault, but all agree it was wrong. Would it still have been wrong if my colleague was a child and not an adult? When does the line of acceptable age to be hit end? Six? Twelve? Twenty-one? Does it make a difference that the person who slapped her was a stranger and not a loving parent? I can't imagine she would feel anything other than embarrassment and resentment, regardless of who slapped her. I agree, she wasn't abused in the technical sense of the word, but she was traumatized. The tour guide did not want her touching the elevator button, which is no different from parents not wanting their child to touch the knobs on the TV. Although I realize this is an isolated incident, it did not deter my colleague from touching an elevator control panel again. Which is exactly my point: if we continuously need to spank our children for them to correct their behaviour, then we haven't effectively taught them an alternative to that behaviour.

Parents may not look upon a spanking as an assault on a child's body, but the child might view it as such. When we spank, the potential to physically hurt is always there. And even if we do not physically hurt our children by spanking, we undoubtedly emotionally harm them. Spanking humiliates and intimidates children. They learn to feel shame and guilt, which can have long-term effects if they are felt often enough. Using spankings to change a child's behaviour is a risky manoeuvre—a fine line between narrowly harming a child today and causing irrevocable emotional damage for tomorrow. If the ultimate goal of discipline is to teach our children, then whether or not the research finds spanking abusive is irrelevant. When we go back to our list of what we want for our children, no one has ever said they wanted their child to feel shame and humiliation. No one has said they wanted their child to fear them. I cannot believe that we learn anything out of fear and intimidation except for maybe how to avoid those people and situations that cause those feelings. Children who learn to avoid become sneaky and dishonest. For these reasons, I have come to the conclusion that spanking is punishment.

> *"I love this book about inventors. It teaches you to learn from your mistakes and misfortunes."*
> *Kohan, age 11*

Natural and logical consequences are the cornerstones of discipline. Ensuring that our children are *accountable* for their behaviour is the mortar that holds together the lessons learned. The foundation we are building for our children through these principles is one that is strong and enduring. Natural consequences happen as a result of a particular action and are in direct correlation to the misdeed. There is really nothing else the parent has to do—the child *naturally* learns that certain behaviours bring about undesirable outcomes. If a child refuses to wear a coat outside, then he will get cold. When he is cold, he is miserable and less likely to enjoy the outdoor activity. If a child leaves his favourite remote control car out on the driveway, and Dad runs over it, or it rains, and the battery gets wet, and it no longer works, then he learns that when you leave your stuff lying around, it can get broken or damaged. The only thing a parent needs to do in these situations is not rescue a child from the learning. If Mom runs to the playground to bring her son his coat, then she has negated the need for her son to make the choice to dress appropriately for the weather the next time. If Dad immediately buys his kid another remote control car, the child will then not learn to take proper care of his belongings. The beauty of natural consequences is that they discipline a child without the parent having to even get involved (except maybe having to help the child through his tears). The child will realize what needs to be done next time to prevent unwanted results.

When I go shopping with my mother and two sisters, I have learned to drive to the mall in my own vehicle. My eldest sister is a marathon shopper. She can spend hours in the same store, deliberating over items that she never ends up buying anyway. She shops from the time the mall opens until it closes. I find this excruciatingly painful – literally. My back aches, my feet hurt, my legs shoot pains up to my head and I become intolerably cranky. The aches and pains are natural consequences to spending hours walking around, shopping. My irritability is most often projected onto my sister and, on more than on one occasion, we ended up quarrelling. I now insist on driving myself so I have the option to leave whenever I feel like it. This way, I prevent World War III between me and my sister, have fun for the hours I do stay and shop and still have energy left over at the end of it all.

When we make mistakes as adults, we have to adhere to the consequences of our actions. If we drink and operate a motorized vehicle, then we lose our licence to drive. If we are consistently late for work, then we can expect a reprimand from our superior and be docked pay. If we don't pay our hydro bill, then our service is cut off. These are real-world consequences to our misbehaviour. Disciplining our children helps groom them for the reality of their futures. They need to be prepared for what can happen when they do something wrong outside the protective walls of their parents' home. In the absence of natural outcomes, *logical consequences* are imposed to teach a child why his behaviour is unacceptable, and they offer alternative ways in which the child should behave. If a young child is banging a toy against a piece of furniture, then the logical thing to do is take the child's toy away. Tell him that banging on your coffee table leaves marks, the toy could get broken and that you play with toys—you do not hit with them. If a toddler takes a crayon to the walls, then you have him help you wash the wall and show him that crayons are only to be used on paper. If a school-age child refuses to do his homework, then he does not move on to another activity before his homework is done. If bedtime rolls around before he has completed his assignment, then you have him realize the consequences his teacher will impose when he shows up at school the next morning with unfinished work. If the school does not take action for incomplete homework, then you send a note to the teacher asking her to discuss with your child how and when he will get caught up, which may mean he will have to stay in for recess. Logical consequences should make sense to the child. They should go hand-in-hand with the child's misbehaviour, so that the relationship between his actions and the consequences of those actions are meaningful to him.

The other piece that is so inherent to the discipline puzzle is getting our children to be *accountable* for their behaviour. It's one thing to correct their behaviour and have them replace it with an acceptable one, but it is not a complete picture until the child learns to take responsibility for his actions. My child was angry at school one day and ripped up his math notebook and was sent to the principal's office. His teacher called me at home to discuss his disrespect of her and of school property. He understood that it was not appropriate for him to become destructive when angry. Together we discussed reasonable suggestions for how he could deal with feelings of frustration and annoyance. Being sent to the principal's office gave him the message that you are not allowed to be disrespectful in class and, if you are, you will lose the privilege of staying there. However, what the principal's office did not address was his destruction of school property or the hurt feelings of his teacher. He needed to be accountable for his behaviour and, in being so, make it right. He wrote a letter of apology to his teacher, recognizing how he had made her feel, stating why it was unacceptable for him to act that way and listing, from what we discussed, how he could more appropriately deal with his anger the next time. He also had to rewrite his math notebook cover to cover. (Lucky for him it was early November so he only had two months worth of material to re-copy.) Through these disciplinary measures, he gained empathy for how his actions had impacted other people. He accepted responsibility and found remorse. With 99 per cent certainty, he will not tear up that math book again, or lip off to his teacher.

> *"Daddy, you should send your brother a card or something. Maybe saying you were sorry for the things you said to him just isn't enough."*
>
> Nolan, age 8

On Christmas Eve day, when our two older children were six and four years of age, I ran upstairs to answer the door, leaving the two of them alone in the basement. It was my best friend, dropping off some gifts. About five minutes after letting her into the house, we heard the sound of breaking glass coming from downstairs. I quickly responded to the noise and found my two boys standing near the TV entertainment unit with golf clubs in their hands. A golf ball had gone through the glass of the cabinet, and it had shattered beneath their feet. Thinking they were in big trouble, they instantly began blaming each other for what had happened, and it was obvious that I was not going to get to the truth of the matter. Frazzled, I couldn't think fast enough to do anything except remove the boys from harm's way and tell them I would need time to think about what I was going to do. They retreated to their rooms, indubitably shaking in their boots, and I continued to visit with my friend.

The boys were too little to help me pick up broken glass. The time spent cleaning up after my friend had gone home allowed me to reflect on the situation. The first thing I had to do was find a better place to store the golf clubs other than the downstairs closet. Discipline is a creative process at the best of times, and I pride myself on utilizing whatever resources are at my disposal. Not unlike the example of our middle child in the mall losing the privilege of seeing Santa, this was Christmas, so I took full advantage of the season's ritual of gift giving to discipline my children. The glass on the entertainment unit needed to be replaced. That would cost money—money we didn't necessarily have during that time of year. The boys weren't very rich either, except for a few coins sitting at the bottom of their piggy banks—not nearly enough to buy and install a new piece of glass. I told the boys that after Christmas they would each need to choose one gift that they had received and give it to their father and me so that we could return the gifts to a store for a refund. The refunded money would go toward paying for the new glass. The gifts had to be of a certain value—candy canes from their stockings would not suffice; it had to be worth 10 dollars or more. On Boxing Day night, after the extended family gift exchange was complete, I was lying in bed snuggling our eldest child. He began to cry and told me that he thought his brother should only have to give up a gift that he truly didn't like. Not fully understanding him, I probed a little bit as to what he meant exactly. He then launched into a blubbery wail and admitted that he was the one who had shot the golf ball through the glass, that his brother hadn't even swung the club. Our eldest child explained that it wasn't fair that his brother had to give up a gift when it wasn't even his brother's fault that the glass got broken.

There are rare moments when our children find the higher meaning in something we have intended to teach. If I could take that moment and put it in a bottle to preserve it, and give it to our son every time he faced a dilemma in his life where moral reasoning could set his soul free, I would never have to worry about disciplining him again. But learning is a lifelong process. Parenting is a never ending journey. In this instance, my husband and I decided that our son's confession and regard for his brother was priceless in comparison to what it would cost to replace the glass. The boys got to keep all of their gifts that Christmas. And the best present my husband and I got was that our six-year-old child had opened the door to developing a conscience, by putting his brother before himself.

8
Self-esteem

"Kohan, you were fantastic out there!
I could really see how hard you were trying."
"You could see that?"

Mother, age 30-something
Kohan, age 5

Self-esteem is not an innate quality. We are not born knowing how we feel about ourselves or what we mean to others. Its development begins in infancy, with the interactions we have with our parents and how we interpret and internalize those relationships. It unfolds with the perceptions of those around us, our experiences and whether or not their outcomes are positive in nature. It is a process of negotiating feelings, physical and mental capabilities and incorporating them all into a definition of who we are. On the map of parenting, it is a fork in the road; one way leads to the development of well-adjusted, self-confident, vital individuals, and the other way leads to the evolution of a person who sees himself and his contribution to the world as worthless. Instilling a healthy self-esteem in our children is the crux of all parenting. When I present to a group of parents on the topic of self-esteem, I use the acronym SELF to help illustrate the behaviours a parent needs to express to their child, so that child will develop a healthy sense of himself: *Support, Empowerment, Love* that is unconditional and *Faith* in their child's capabilities are the essentials required to raise children with a sense of belonging and self-worth. Through a consistent showing of the SELF parenting behaviours, children get positive reinforcement of specific attributes. These characteristics also fit within the SELF acronym: when a child is supported, he is *Strengthened*; when he is empowered, he feels *Encouraged*; when he knows that he is loved unconditionally, he learns to *Love* himself; and when his parents have faith in him, he is *Fulfilled* as a human being.

This last chapter in *Out of the Mouths of Babes* is the sum of all its parts. The message throughout has been to develop an understanding for how a child sees and feels about a given situation, to listen to and respect your child's point of view, and to attune to a child's individual needs and personality, and parent him accordingly. Parenting from a child's perspective is essential to fostering a healthy self-esteem. When we adhere to the principles of attachment parenting, we create an environment that is supportive and empowering. We allow our children to explore and take risks, make mistakes and learn from them. Based on our child's individual strength of character, we set him up for success so he will acquire confidence in his abilities. We love our children unconditionally by seeing their misbehaviour as opportunities for them to learn and grow. We guide them through their experiences and empower them to make decisions that are right for them. We set limits and boundaries, teach them conflict resolution and have faith that they will learn right from wrong. As a result, our children grow to love themselves and the world around them. They make choices that are right for them because it is what they know how to do. They recognize their strengths and limitations and easily gravitate toward living an authentic life—one that is rich in health and happiness. Therefore, when they go out into the world and claim their own accomplishments, they will have us, their parents, to thank for their success, because through our teachings, they learned to believe in themselves.

"Mommy, when I was born, did you love me right away? Like, what if I was a stranger and just showed up at your door—would you know that you loved me then?"

Nolan, age 6

Communication is the tool that enables the SELF parenting behaviours and facilitates parenting from a child's perspective. Through verbal messages and nonverbal gestures, we share our thoughts and feelings with our children. By listening, we can ascertain how our children are thinking and feeling. Communication promotes the reciprocal exchange of intended meaning, whether the meaning is in the content of the words we use or not. Body language, voice intonation and facial expressions also play an integral part in how our messages are received.

When I give a presentation on the topic of self-esteem, I request that members of the audience play a modified version of the game *Hedbanz.* Eight to ten adult participants are asked to come to the front of the class and pick a topic of controversy to discuss. Subject matter chosen most often is abortion, legalizing marijuana or the safety of guns. On their heads, I adorn crowns of construction paper with something written such as *tell me I'm stupid, yell at me, ridicule me, praise me, tell me I'm right, tell me I'm wrong, encourage me, ignore me, question me, or agree with me.* The volunteers are not aware of what is scribed on their own individual tiaras but are instructed that, during their conversation, they are only allowed to respond to the person speaking in accordance with what that person's headband says. It's an exaggerated way to show parents the messages we give our children by the way we communicate with them. The conversation seldom lasts longer than five or ten minutes before I have made my point. I have witnessed participants turn red with shame, become enraged when they felt they were not being heard, tell me that the game was ridiculous and refuse to continue. I've even seen some cry. Afterward, I always ask the parents what they thought was written on their paper crowns. Nine times out of ten, they guess right. I ask parents then to just imagine the damage we do to our children's feeling of self-worth when we are constantly ridiculing or artificially praising them. When we are continually pessimistic toward a child, we give the message that that child doesn't matter. Children cannot feel good about themselves if their expressed ideas and feelings are always ignored or negatively challenged. They will not feel encouraged to try new things and acquire new skills, if their efforts and opinions are constantly dismissed for wrong. Nor will they have a real sense of their strengths and limitations if they have been given false praise for everything they say and do. In this instance, they learn to blame others for their failures because they do not see themselves as anything but great. When they become overinflated with an unrealistic view of themselves, they make it difficult for other people to like them and, as a result, will often confront being rejected. Feelings derived from humiliation and rejection only get internalized over time. These feelings manifest in negative, attention-seeking and mischievous behaviours. The consequence is a child who grows up with low self-esteem and becomes an adult who is at risk for substance abuse, dysfunctional relationships, lack of job satisfaction and depression.

> *"He called me a baby in front of my friend. I was embarrassed. He has to know how that made me feel, and I don't want to talk to him again until he understands."*
>
> *Nolan, age 9*

The messages our children receive from us are not only contained in *what* we say, but also in *how* we say it. When our youngest child comes to us with his latest drawing, we take the time to study it, tell him that we love the colours he chose and ask him about the story behind it. We comment on the detail he put into it and I post it on the fridge or my husband takes it to work for his office. Our son gets the message that we recognize and appreciate the effort he puts into making pictures and that we see him as a hard worker who pays a lot of attention to colour and detail. In contrast, if we barely took the time to look at his work of art but said in passing that we thought it was beautiful, then our son would most likely feel discounted, regardless of the compliment the word "beautiful" was suppose to give. This son of ours actually is quite adept at drawing—it is hard not to overly praise his efforts. Consequently, he has come to know (and possibly rely on) how much we like his artistic ability; it's the first thing he uses against us when he's angry. Emphatically, he will tell us "no more pictures for you" whenever he can't get his own way.

> *"Those two are fighting because Sarah is jealous that*
> *Tommy has been playing with that toy for so long."*
> *Kohan, age 4*

Our meaning must be intended in all aspects of communication so the message cannot be misconstrued. It's not an easy task. Sometimes life gets in the way of being cognizant of how we are communicating, and the messages we send give way to meaning that was never intended. It's important then to clarify understanding with our children. Have them repeat back what they heard and tell how they feel about it. In order for them to do this, they first need a broad vocabulary of feelings. I laugh sometimes when I hear well-meaning parents insist their toddlers "use their words" to handle peer disputes. *What words?* It is highly unlikely that these little people with a repertoire of about 36 phrases or less than 100 words, know how to say *frustrated, angry, annoyed, jealous, provoked* or *bothered*. What they know how to do when they are feeling any of these ways is to hit, bite, scratch, kick, scream or cry. It's a survival tactic. From the time our children are babes in arms, we need to be labelling their feelings for them so they can inventory a number of different ways in which to express themselves. Once the capacity for language expands, they will already know words to communicate their feelings. So the next time they are asked to use their words, they will have the right one on hand to explain exactly their point of view. This also helps them to recognize the feelings of others, so communication is less misunderstood.

So, how we talk to one another can clean a sword or bloody it. Once, while working in child and adolescent psychiatry, I was sent to the emergency room to assess a 16-year-old girl admitted for overdose of her mother's prescription medicine. This family had a long-standing history within the system and had burned a lot of bridges along the way. It was my first encounter with them, and I was forewarned by many well-meaning colleagues that the mother of the teenager was belligerent, uncooperative and vile and that I would be wasting my time interviewing the young girl if the mother was present. I met with my co-workers exact description of this mother upon entering the room. She immediately began telling me the flaws of the mental health system and the wrongdoings of every intervention worker assigned to their case. She chastised her daughter in colourful language and berated the hospital staff for their ill treatment of her since her daughter's admission. I allowed her the opportunity to vent, acknowledging her vehemence through a nod of my head or a vocal purr of encouragement. When she had exhausted herself, leaving an opening for me to respond, I quietly said, "I can't imagine how difficult this must be for you." After all, her child did just try to commit suicide. That cannot be easy for anyone. My validation of her experience was enough to kick-start our therapeutic alliance.

I worked with this family for over a year. At that time, I was the only mental health professional committed to helping them. We had so much to do to repair relationships in the community and bring others back on board to assist this family. The mother was encouraged to contract with other agency services when she understood how they would help her. She was empowered to parent differently, starting with communication. Together, she and her daughter had to relearn how to speak to one another; it was like learning an entirely different language. They began communicating in a mutually respectful manner. The daughter began to feel valued, and the mother became more confident in her ability to parent. At the time I closed their case, the daughter was back living with her mother full-time, and she had returned to school. The mother barely resembled the woman I had met that first day in hospital. She was more in control of herself and better equipped to take care of her daughter. The turn of events for this family started because I listened. The mother, after years of feeling disdained and rejected, felt heard, with her experience validated. Therein, communication was the catalyst for change.

"Nolan! Just look at this math test. Way to go!"
"Yeah, I feel really good about it."
Mother, age 40-something
Nolan, age 9

Our eldest son used to be a reluctant writer. It was a real concern. In school, when it came time for writing exercises, he would sit and waste time—in an attention deficit disorder kind of way. The teacher was so perplexed when, after given enough time to complete an assignment, he had nothing accomplished. He would waste time staring out the window or fidgeting with his pencil. If homework writing assignments were due, he would conveniently misplace the notebooks or paper that supposedly had the instructions or half the assignment already written on them. This is a child who has such a creative imagination. He's an inventor of ideas and loves to tell stories. But, for the life of us, we could not get him to write any of it down. We had numerous meetings with his teacher and tried everything to inspire his creativity to come out on paper. After completing grade two, his teacher assigned him a summer writing project where he was encouraged to write a daily journal. The teacher said she delighted in hearing his stories of being up at the cottage for the summer, and, because she thought she would not be his teacher the following year, she would appreciate it if he would keep a log of his holiday activities that she could read. (As it turned out, she did teach him the next year. She was assigned the next grade and, having felt like she was not "finished" with our son yet, requested to take him with her.) It was a daily struggle to get him to write in his journal. There were days where the act itself did not seem worth it. But through many fights and tears, he managed to write 72 entries of tales of him swimming and frog hunting and roasting marshmallows at campfires.

At the beginning of the next school year, our son put a bow around his tiny little book and presented it to this teacher. She was elated, to say the least. She took it from him with such care and wrote back to our son what experiences she enjoyed reading about the most. He was thrilled with her enthusiasm. One of the things we recognized through this activity was his inability to spell words correctly. The same words were misspelled over and over again; he had great difficulty learning from his mistakes. With the aid of his teacher, we were able to put together a program that would assist him with his impediment to spelling. His teacher the following year, having been apprised of the situation, told our son from the start that she didn't care about his spelling. That she had been teaching for 30 years and would be able to read anything he wrote for her. Through the wisdom of these two teachers, our son has become a budding author. He now has a notebook he carries around with him; when inspired, he jots down ideas for stories, comic strips and poems. He has also taken a keen interest in reading books about piracy and adventures in the wilderness, and they excite and ignite his creativity even further.

This past summer, while vacationing at the cottage, I had seen an advertisement in the local paper for a writing workshop that was taking place as part of a community summer festival. I had decided that I would attend. To our amazement, my eldest child asked if he could come along. When we got there, I asked

108

the facilitator if it was okay for my 11-year-old to participate because I wasn't sure if there would be an age restriction. It was perfectly fine for him to take part. He was the only child among 15 adults. The workshop was an exercise in free association. We were instructed to pull a page from the dictionary and write about the first word that leapt out at us. We were given 20 minutes to write and 20 minutes to edit. Two years ago, that amount of time for writing would have sent my son into a tailspin. Through the editing exercise, I saw him use the dictionary to look up misspelled words, and he carefully rewrote what he had produced in good copy on a fresh sheet of paper. No one was going to be marking this assignment so his interest in doing well was astounding.

When we came together as a group to share with one another what we had written, he was the first to volunteer his work. He wrote the poem *Uncomfortable Things*. His confidence in reading aloud was inspiring. At the conclusion of the workshop, he was inundated with questions about his writing ability. He gave credit to the two teachers who never gave up on him and who told him that his writing was more important than his capacity to spell. I was in awe of his maturity in giving credence to his teachers. I hadn't fully appreciated how much he recognized those two individuals as having helped him. It was also the first time I had ever heard him verbalize that, once he knew he was not going to get penalized for spelling mistakes, it was easier for him to write. Because of how those teachers communicated with him, his strength in imagination and creativity was nurtured. He acknowledges his weakness in spelling, which only assists him to manage it. Through caring persistence, supportive encouragement and a belief in his ability to do it, our son learned to write. And he's pretty darn good at it too—if I do say so myself.

Uncomfortable Things
It is uncomfortable to be sprayed by a skunk,
It is uncomfortable to sit in a small wooden trunk,
I find it uncomfortable to sleep on a fluffy pillow,

> *Or on a bed that is too hard.*
> *It is uncomfortably scary to stare from a window that's barred,*
> *What is uncomfortable for me, may not be uncomfortable for you,*
> *So appreciate the differences between us,*
> *I really hope you do.*
>
> Kohan, age 11

A healthy self-esteem is not obtained solely through the acquisition of success. We cannot protect our children from experiencing failure. In fact, we can use our children's failures and disappointments to teach them a great deal about resilience and buoyancy of spirit. Self-esteem is an aspect of our character that will fluctuate from time to time. Throughout life, we are challenged to put the perception of ourselves and how others see us at equilibrium. Any number of situational crises can alter the view a person has of himself. For adults, circumstances such as divorce, the loss of a job, financial difficulties, or being in love with someone who does not share the same feelings, can all negatively impact our self-esteem. Children can experience feelings of self-doubt if they are struggling to keep up in school, having peer difficulties or experiencing discord within their families. It will be through these trying times, not their windfalls, when they learn about the instinct to survive, the strength of spirit and just how resourceful they can be.

My mother used to say to me, "What doesn't kill you will only make you stronger." I have felt as though I was going to die on a few occasions (figuratively speaking), but in each case, I came through with a renewed sense of who I am. In every adversity, there are valuable lessons to learn about ourselves. Instead of trying to protect our children from the harsh realities of failure, we need to help them identify the lessons that lie within those failures. Teach them adaptive coping and conflict resolution skills. Encourage them to draw upon their strengths to lift their spirits. As they navigate their way through intervals of difficulty, guide them, but don't rescue. Be underfoot to catch them when they fall, and empower them to get back up. Allow them the opportunity to overcome the negative assaults on their self-esteem when they are young, so they will know what to do to persevere when they are faced with a crisis when they are older.

> *"Nobody likes me. Nobody wants to play with me because I'm stupid."*
>
> Talen, age 4

Our eldest son spent one afternoon in the backyard with his grandfather, learning how to bat a baseball, catch a pop fly and stop a grounder. Grandpa offered our boy a lot of encouragement, and he felt pretty good about what he was able to learn in such a short period of time. Inspired, our son decided to try out for the school baseball team. It was the first year he was eligible to play. His enthusiasm for wanting to make the team was motivating, but unfortunately, it did not match his ability and skill level. Tossing a ball around for one afternoon in the backyard does not a baseball player make. The first day of tryouts, there must have been over 60 kids out on the field—many of them older experienced players. He was heartbroken when his name didn't appear on the roster at the conclusion of tryouts. Knowing it before it happened, my husband and I could do nothing to protect him from the disappointment. For the next few days, the scenario played out like this: He first blamed the coach for not giving him a fair chance to show his stuff. Then he said it was only the popular guys in school who got picked. Then, in an attempt to minimize his feelings, he said that he really didn't like the sport that much anyway, so it really didn't bother him. It was plain to see that he was upset, and his self-esteem altered.

My sister graduated at the top of her class. She climbed her way through the ranks and went on to have a very rewarding career in management for almost 20 years. As a result of a massive restructuring where the city amalgamated the municipalities within the region, my sister's position became obsolete, and she was essentially demoted to a lower classification. She went to work within an environment where people were just as unhappy about their forced situation as she was. The negativity surrounding my sister and her co-workers took on a life of its own, and they began manufacturing contempt for one another. The interpersonal conflict that arose was outrageous, and it made going to work everyday unbearable. The work itself wasn't even enough to keep my sister's spirits up. The new position did very little to kindle the fire within. Her skills were underutilized, and her authority to make decisions within a department had been revoked. She felt stagnant. As opportunities came along for her to reclaim her status, her negative attitude sabotaged her chances. Alarmingly, she began to find reasons in other people for her lack of achievement. It was not surprising when she succumbed to the environment and lost sight of her purpose. The toxic culture of her workplace gravely affected her self-esteem. A formerly vivacious, passionate, innovative person, she became cynical and self-loathing. To her family, my sister was barely recognizable.

In the game of life, my sister's experience parallels my son's in how their self-esteem was negatively impacted by a situational setback. They both thought their contribution to the team unwanted; consequently, their sense of belonging was threatened. They both questioned their competence and began doubting their abilities to succeed. In an attempt to protect themselves from the harsh realities of failure, they redirected the blame and took on attitudes of indifference. But these feelings were temporary. Through the love and support of others, my sister and her nephew were both empowered to persevere. My sister was able to take ownership for what part she played in the downward spiral of her career. She gathered the strength she knew was within her and found the courage to make changes. My son realized that if you want something badly enough, then you have to practice at it, and even at that, every now and then you have to accept that you can't be good at everything. The following year, he tried out for the basketball team, but before stepping out onto the court, he got prepared. He learned the rules of the game, shot hoops out on the front drive and talked with his father about strategic plays. With a renewed sense of themselves, my sister landed her dream job, and my son made the basketball team.

At the conclusion of my sister's ordeal, my family hosted an afternoon celebration in her honour, congratulating her on her new job. I wrote the following poem as part of a tribute to her. In retrospect, it helps put into perspective the concept of self-esteem and how it rises and falls through the peaks and valleys of life—how a person can overcome an assault on his character when love and support are behind him. And how, when the foundation of one's inner core is solid, the self will return to it, ready for more.

Fly

Nurtured by the ties that bind
In a nesting home of three,
Surrounded by a love so strong,
There's you, there's her, and there's me.

We watched you learn to fly with grace,
How you would spread your wings and soar.
I wanted so much to emulate you,
So I watched you all the more.

Your wingspan brushed the sky with colour,
And the people looked up in awe.
You painted images inviting leisure,
Giving pleasure, to those who saw.

To watch you rise was a marvellous thing.
From the depths of our hearts we'd cry
Out loud, that you would hear our cheer.
Fly, my sister, fly!

When having such a splendid journey,
A storm intercepted your flight.
You fell amid the menacing clouds,
Then you faded out of sight.

Our nest of three was down by one.
Leaving the two of us asking, "Why?"
We wished to heal your broken wing,
And give flight another try.

Try you did, and falter so
But the ties that bind made sure
You would grace the sky on mended wing,
Precisely, as you were.

So when you flew, we held our breath,
Then whispered a prayer with a sigh:
Please, Lord, take good care of her.
Fly, my sister, Fly!

The belief that we both have in you,
Was often stronger than your own.
And when you swore you could not go on,
We gave you faith on loan.

With mended wing and strength of heart,
You forged ahead and flew.
Navigating through many storms,
Your spirit was renewed.

You learned to fly a different way,
A little more cautious than before,
Passion and grace you still possess,
Assenting, you strive for more.

So ready yourself; spread your wings.
Go paint your canvas sky.
We'll be here cheering for you,
Fly, my sister, fly!

> *"All right, this is too loud. All little people*
> *are to go and play in their rooms."*
> *"I am not a little people; I am a big-little*
> *people. I am as big as a miracle!"*
> *Father, age 30-something*
> *Madelyn, age 3*

When I was growing up, I consistently got the message that I could do and be anything I wanted. But it wasn't as broad a belief as it sounds. My parents encouraged my interests and nurtured my talents. They helped me discover my strengths and improve upon my deficiencies, and they guided me in the direction of choosing a career path that was within my scope of capabilities. So when I chose nursing and then diversified into psychiatry, it wasn't out of the realm of possibilities for me. When I told my parents about wanting to write a parenting book, my father reminded me of the poetry and short stories I had written when I was younger. He told me that he had always held the belief that I was a talented writer and that if I wanted to write a book, he had no doubt that I would. My mother said that I had a gift and that I was a wise parent and should share my experiences through my writing. So it comes to pass, my parent's belief in my ability to write *Out of the Mouths of Babes* came long before I knew I could do it. It's only fitting that the words to conclude this final chapter should be: Thanks, Mom and Dad.

More from
Out of the Mouths of Babes

"Who do you think invented the potato?"
"George Washington probably."

Alex, age 8
Keldan, age 8

Passing gas while sitting on the toilet:
"Talen, do you have to poo?"
"No. I'm just breathing like a dolphin."

Father, age 40-something
Talen, age 4

"Mommy, I know you don't feel well enough to go to church today. I figure we could just take time to pray during the day."

Nolan, age 8

"What does G-A-Y mean?"
After receiving an explanation: "Well, God must make people that way for a reason. If I was gay, you would still love me, right?"

Nolan, age 7

"When the light shines through the clouds, then I can sleep in your bed and snuggle you?"

Talen, age 3½

"*School is not open today, but Grandma and Papa's house is always open.*"

Talen, age 4

"*Daddy, I thought you said we were going to the liquorice store? I don't see any liquorice.*"
"*No, Nolan, it's the liquor store.*"

Nolan, age 6
Father, age 40-something

"*Dana, you should come home with Uncle Rob. I don't have any little girls at my house.*"
"*Don't be silly; I need a girl to take care of me.*"

Uncle Rob, age 40-something
Dana, age 3

"*Ryan, what do you think of my socks?*"
"*They make you look fat.*"

Mother, age 40-something
Ryan, age 4

"*I don't want to get older and have old eyes like Grandma.*"

Talen, age 3

"*I don't like the sound of the fan. The only sound I like is the ringing of the doorbell when it's the pizza man.*"

Nolan, age 7

"*Boys don't have babies, Keldan.*"
Yes, they do, Daddy said girls have eggs, and boys have Sea Monkeys."

Mother, age 30-something
Keldan, age 6

"You're the best mommy I didn't have."
                                    Talen, age 3

*"Grandma, you have done just about everything;
you might as well be dead."*
                                    Nolan, age 6½

*While digging for clams: "For God's sake, Grandma,
just get it in the bucket!"*
                                    Kohan, age 5

*"The Easter Bunny came into our house and left
eggs, but he didn't poop on the floor."*
                                    Ava, age 2½

"Mommy, tell Nolan to stop pointing his penis at me."
"Mommy, my can't! It's standing up on its own."
                                    Kohan, age 5
                                    Nolan, age 3

*"When I was sleeping, I heard the sun say to the
rain 'go away rain, it's my turn.' And see, Mommy,
the sun is out today."*
                                    Talen, age 4

*(The day before, Mom's car wouldn't start so Dad
put in gas-line antifreeze to get it going.)*
*"Mom, you'd better make sure you put in some of
that ass line panty freeze, or your car might not
start again."*
                                    Ryan, age 4

After being invited by a friend to attend a party with a Brownie group:
"Mom, when do I get to go the muffin festival?"

Madelyn, age 6

"Noah, would you like a grilled cheese for lunch?"
"No, I wan' boy cheese."

neighbour, age 30-something
Noah, age 3

"I asked the girls if they wanted to meet my grandma. I told them she looks like a turtle."
"What do you mean, a turtle?"
"Grandma's neck is all crinkly and loose like a turtle's!"

Talen, age 4
Mother, age 30-something

"Talen, I hear you think Grandma looks like a turtle. Do I look like a turtle?"
"No, Papa, you look like a giraffe because of all the brown spots you have on you."

Talen, age 4
Papa, age 70-something

(Grandma and Grandpa were away on a trip over Thanksgiving, and my sisters were arguing over who should say grace at the turkey supper.)
"Well, you wouldn't have this problem if you would have invited Grandpa to dinner."

Keldan, age 10

"Don't touch him penis (the dog). If you touch it, it will grow big. I don't like it when my penis grows big. It gets too bouncy."
Talen, age 4¾

"Mommy did you know that we are made of meat?"
"I suppose we are. And who made us?"
"God did. Well, He's a good builder of meat!"
Talen, age 5
Mother, age 40-something

(The sign read "hiring for all shifts, apply within.")
"Those poor people who have to work all shifts, they never get a break"
Julia, age 9

"Talen, you were screaming outside like you always do. I didn't know you were screaming for help. I didn't know you were hurt."
"Well, how 'bout you come into the backyard and watch me. If you were there Nolan never would have been mean to me!"
Mother, age 40-something
Talen, age 5

About the Author

Dyan Eybergen, a paediatric psychiatric nurse, has more than ten years experience working as a therapist and parent educator. Dyan and her family were guests on the cable television show "For Kids Sake," along with parenting expert Barbara Coloroso. Eybergen resides in Ontario, Canada, with her husband and three sons.

Inquiries regarding Dyan Eybergen and speaking opportunities can be directed to www.childperspectiveparenting.com

Bibliography

Ainsworth, M., M. C. Blehar, E. Waters, and S. Wahl. *Patterns of Attachment.* Hillsdale, NJ: L. Erlbaum, 1978.

Asher, D. 2001. Where did I come from? Here's how to tackle those tricky first questions about sex. *Parents.* 76:163–64. http://www.askdrsears.com/html/2/T022500.asp.

Bowlby, J. *A Secure Base: Parent-Child Attachment and Healthy Human Development.* New York: Basic Books, 1988.

———. *Children Apart: How Parents Can Help Young Children Cope with Being away from the Family.* New York: Pantheon Books, 1973.

Brazelton, T. B., and B. G. Cramer. *The Earliest Relationship: Parents, Infants, and the Drama of Early Attachment.* Reading, MA: Wesley, Addison, 1990.

Brazelton, T. B. and J. D. Sparrow. *Understanding Sibling Rivalry: The Brazelton Way.* Cambridge, MA: Da Capo Press, 2005.

———. *Toilet Training: The Brazelton Way.* Cambridge, MA: Da Capo Press, 2004.

Chess, S., and A. Thomas. *Temperament: Theory and Practice.* New York: Brunner/Mazel, 1996.

Christophersen, E. Time in before time-out: Time-out from positive reinforcement? *Parenting.com. 2003.* http://www.parenthood.com/articles.html?article_id=4237.

Christophersen, E. and S. M. VanScoyoc. What makes time-out work (and fail)? *dbpeds.org.* 2007. http://www.dbpeds.org/articles/detail.cfm?TextID=%20739.

Coloroso, B.. *Kids Are Worth It!: Giving Your Child the Gift of Inner Discipline. Rev. ed.* Toronto: Penguin Group (Canada), 2001.

Ferber, R.. *Solve Your Child's Sleep Problems. Rev. and expanded ed.* New York: Fireside Book, 2006.

Fraiberg, S. H. *The Magic Years: Understanding and Handling the Problems of Early Childhood.* New York: Fireside Book, 1996.

Gross-Loh, C. *The Diaper-Free Baby: The Natural Toilet Training Alternative.* New York: Regan, 2007.

Lieberman, A. F. *The Emotional Life of the Toddler.* New York: The Free Press, 1993.

Maccoby, E. E. *Social Development: Psychological Growth and the Parent-Child Relationship.* New York: Harcourt Brace Jovanovich, 1980.

Martens, M. Reconsidering the research on spanking. *Today's Family News.* 2004. http://www.fotf.ca/tfn/family/articles/Spanking_research.htm.

Martens Miller, P. *Sex Is Not a Four-Letter Word: Talking Sex with Your Children Made Easier.* New York: The Crossword Publishing Company, 1994.

Phillips, A. M. *Toilet Learning: The Picture Book Technique for Children and Parents.* Boston: Little, Brown, 1978.

Pincus, D. and J. Otis. Fears, Phobias and Anxiety. *The Child Anxiety Network. 2007* http://www.childanxiety.net/Fears_Phobias_Anxiety.htm.

Reeve, J. "Mommy I'm scared": Understanding children's fears. *Lifespan.* 2007. http://www.lifespan.org/services/childhealth/parenting/fears.htm.

Shaver, P. R., C. Hazan, and D. Bradshaw. 1988. Love as attachment: The integration of three behavioural systems. In R. J. Sternberg and M. Barnes (Eds.), *Anatomy of Love.* 68–99.

Spicer, S. 2003. A real eye-opener: Putting to rest some popular myths about kids and sleep. *Today's Parent: Canada's Parenting Magazine.* 20: 94–98.

Spock, B. Dr. *Spock's The First Two Years: The Emotional and Physical Needs of Children from Birth to Age Two.* New York: Pocket Books, 2001.

Stern, D. N. *The First Relationship: Infant and Mother.* Cambridge, MA: Harvard University Press, 2002.

Thomas, A. and S. Chess. *Temperament and Development.* New York: Brunner/Mazel, 1977.

Printed in the United States
136531LV00001B/4/P